MIND DEFINITION

DEFINING MBA PRINCIPLES FOR CAREER SUCCESS IN THE DIGITAL AGE

VIN B. BITTENCOURT

Distribution by Bublish, Inc.
Published by Business Institute of California Publishing

ISBN: 978-1-647045-75-3 (paperback)
ISBN: 978-1-647045-76-0 (eBook)

Contents

Preface

I t's a fact of life—not everything can be controlled. But of the things that can, perhaps no other is more important than your professional future. Your career is a foundational vehicle to many other areas in your life, where you not only find livelihood and prosperity but much of your sense of identity and self-worth. And while there are many avenues for purpose and self-worth unrelated to work or career status, most of us invest years in preparation and training before assuming a productive, remunerated role in society.

The world is more emotional than rational. Life-changing decisions are more visceral than cognitive. Yet, one element that all successful people have in common is a sense of purpose. Successful people move strategically toward a goal, and although not all of the decisions they make are necessarily smart, most are measured and have a target. *Mind Definition: Defining MBA Principles for Career Success in the Digital Age* is a manual on making wise career decisions. My purpose for creating this manual is simple: I wanted to craft a relatable, accessible road map with timeless principles to help all working professionals, from the uninitiated to the midcareer worker looking for a change, to those who know they want more and have finally decided to think strategically about their careers—either because their clock is ticking or because they've become fully aware of massive technological, economic, and societal changes in the 2020s.

The networked age is shattering the world of work. Companies now generate more revenue with fewer people while designing human capital strategies to attract, develop, and retain unique professionals for key roles where well-defined skills, experiences, and competencies are the norm.

Career tracks have become increasingly more niched, creating demand for a combination of technical and interpersonal skills. Due to this demand, companies are looking for T-shaped individuals—experts who can navigate the weeds of a subject while moving laterally, stepping comfortably into different areas.

In summary, companies in the digital age not only want people with deep-seated domain knowledge and training, but equally calibrated personality, character, and flexibility, essential ingredients for navigating a world that requires constant evolution and adaptability.

While no one becomes a T-shaped professional by accident, everyone can achieve excellence with focused preparation and training—or, simply put, a career strategy. With this premise, I embarked on a three-year research and personal documentation journey to write *Mind Definition*: *Defining MBA Principles for Career Success in the Digital Age.*

If there was ever an age to be in control and to secure a professional future of endless possibilities for yourself, that age is now. With companies too busy fighting for survival and the velocity of transformations catching schools and training programs off guard, the responsibility to manage your career is exclusively yours.

Mind Definition: Defining MBA Principles for Career Success in the Digital Age brings you a classic MBA lexicon on career management. The book shares meaningful insights that combine theory and practice on actions, behaviors, and choices that work in real life, not just things that look impressive on paper. While I comb through the traditional business school curriculum to bring you the best and the freshest on career management, I steer clear of the sugar-coated platitudes you often find in academia and media. Instead, I focus on practical pointers you can apply immediately.

Despite its optimistic and positive tone, this book is not a feel-good guide. Instead, it invites you to take responsibility for things you can control. Here, you'll learn more about the hidden truths senior leadership isn't allowed to share—the dirty secrets on how to get to the top of every career and profession, tailored and contextualized for the digital age.

From Valet to MBA: A Personal Career Journey Perspective

My professional trajectory in the United States started after moving from Porto Alegre, Brazil to Los Angeles, California in 2005. It involved many service jobs at the school of hard knocks: parking cars, delivering pizza, and pushing luggage at boutique hotels, all while attending a community college, before I finally jumped onto a corporate career track that led to an MBA.

Since then, a lot has happened. In addition to managing projects and cross-functioning teams for global organizations, I experienced firsthand the rise of artificial intelligence, then the mobile, cloud, and big data platform revolutions that came to dictate the future of work.

Over the years, whether working in entertainment or in professional service industries, I've had the privilege of supporting many of the world's largest corporations. In doing so, I've witnessed the drastic technological evolution this era has become famous for. But while this exposure has granted me valuable insights on what it takes to succeed professionally, it doesn't make me a career expert, merely someone who's navigating the same treacherous waters of professional growth that most digital-age workers do in this Wild West of transformations.

Still, with almost two decades of corporate experience and the benefit of hindsight, I can view the rights and wrongs of my career under the microscope of the principles presented here. From my time parking cars, dreaming of a better future, to my present as an educator forging the next generation of leaders, entrepreneurs, and career professionals, there are many lessons to share. The result is this book, where I bring you what I believe to be the golden nuggets of career success in a no-holds-barred exposé. For instance, the expectations most employers have but rarely articulate; qualifiers that hiring managers consider during the interview process; and all the secret and not-so-secret factors influencing hiring and promotion decisions.

You will also be introduced to the Dream Career Canvas, an in-depth and exclusive framework of essential steps to becoming a world-class professional in the digital age. The Canvas presents skills and competencies that will turn you into a powerful complement to machines and artificial systems by walking you through five modules: 1) People and Political; 2) Communication; 3) Original Thinking; 4) Leadership; and 5) Technical Domain Expertise.

Some realizations about combining a classic MBA curriculum with real-life business experiences from this book: success in work life is more about relationships and fit than dedication and talent. Likewise, nothing is more important than being in the right place, with the right team, at the right time. Ultimately, professional success is about connecting with people, building social and political capital, and working with a purpose. It rests on self-awareness—knowing yourself and your strengths—and never settling for anything less than projects that utilize your best individual traits.

Whether you're a beginner, already have battle scars, or are at a midcareer tipping point, this manual will make a difference in your journey. Many people consider MBA programs the ultimate solution for career advancement, and they can be—but I recommend you take a self-discovery journey first to define the contributions you want to make. This book will lead you in that direction with a series of original insights, an analysis of the world of work, and how you should position yourself within it.

MBA Degrees Are Not for Everyone— But They Can Help a Lot of People

The average tuition cost among the top twenty-five business schools in the United States surpasses $195,000 for a full-time, two-year MBA program.[1] As a result, a career strategy module—a staple of every elite MBA—has a stand-alone price of at least $9,750 (with tuition costs broken down into individual class units, 60 units total for a program, and an average of 3 units per class). That's just its present value; this estimated cost doesn't include the value of future earnings, promotions, and subsequent career progress that comes from adopting the lessons and strategies of these modules, or the fulfillment of finding roles that complement your unique strengths—which is arguably something impossible to put a price tag on.

A typical MBA career module takes you through a series of proven psychological, behavioral, and communication assessments to define your areas of excellence. Now, for a fraction of the cost, you can gain much of the same insights through *Mind Definition: Defining MBA Principles for Career Success in the Digital Age.* Moreover, the book immerses you in foundational concepts of elite MBA curricula, giving you exposure to problem-solving and strategic thinking frameworks for an inside scoop on what an MBA program can look like. Tools in communication, leadership, and resource management are some of the exclusive items an MBA education delivers that are still relevant in a tech-centric economy. Here, you'll find an introduction to them.

Overall, at the end of this reading, you will have a better idea as to whether an MBA is a viable option for you based on your aspirations and career goals. For that, we will contrast the marketing promises of business schools with MBA graduates' actual outcomes, profiling the groups that fare better on average in terms of personal satisfaction and professional growth.

Technology creates an uneven playing field in which average skills suffer and extraordinary skills rule. Thriving in the digital age takes resilience, as the knowledge economy rewards self-managed, resourceful, and goal-oriented people infinitely more. In the end, finding a way to identify and develop your personal strengths depends on you and your willingness to conduct an honest assessment of what you bring to the table. This requires a critical lens, both in studying yourself and in studying what is happening on the world stage. Some people say the future is the enemy of the unprepared. After reading this book, you won't be.

Introduction

THE DIGITAL DIVIDE REQUIRES A WHOLE NEW MINDSET

Welcome to the digital divide—the age where artificial intelligence and software dictate the future of work. Estimates reveal that over 50 percent of today's jobs will get completely transformed or cease to exist in the 2020s.[2] Hope is not a strategy in the machine age's professional world. Predictable and stable corporate career tracks are gone, the responsibility to manage your career is yours, and the best advice for professionals in the robot-accelerated era of the twenty-first century is: *Make sure you're on the right side of Moore's Law.*

Here's a universal truth about work: most people have jobs; some people have careers; few people have a true calling. Which do you have? If you are to find purpose, prosperity, and meaning in life, you must at least aim for a career—and that requires a solid vision, preparation, and smart choices. Beyond having a game plan, every person must operate within the three "must-haves" of every career acceleration: 1) the right company; 2) the right boss; and 3) the right assignments. It's absolutely critical to find this magical triad, as a person's growth and earning potential are directly related to the quality of the people and the projects one contributes to. Most people understand they get paid for their knowledge and skills. What they forget is that neither knowledge nor skills are measured in time or years of experience; they are measured in the *quality* and *impact* of projects and assignments—something the language of business calls *results*.

Either you operate within the realm of excellence—by working with the right company, the right boss, and on the right projects—or you don't. Either you have quality experiences and meaningful projects on your portfolio, or you don't. In the end, that's the difference between average and stellar careers. Whenever the must-haves of career acceleration are not in place, no amount of talent or drive can compensate.

Because companies in the world post-digital divide are too busy fighting for survival, they don't have the time and resources to develop workers. That makes you the CEO of your career—the only one in charge of positioning yourself favorably in this tech-centered, networked economy. Refuse the role, and you risk becoming a fatality.

THE WORLD POST–DIGITAL DIVIDE: SIMPLE OR COMPLEX?

With the rapid expansion of computer power, digitization, and networks as primary economic growth engines, odds are that you will soon work for a technology company, if you aren't already. Regardless of the industry, business models will become tech-centric across the board. As of this writing, the latest Standard & Poor's 500 Index shows that five of the world's largest companies by market value are in tech. Apple ($1.5 trillion) is listed as the most valuable company, followed by Microsoft ($1.4 trillion), Amazon ($1.3 trillion), Alphabet ($992 billion), and Facebook ($671 billion).

Staggering valuations indeed, considering they are post-pandemic numbers. These companies are exceptions to what is perhaps one of the most devastating economic crises of the last ninety years, where hundreds of thousands of traditional businesses and industries have folded, and millions of workers having been laid off or let go altogether. Yet, tech companies are not just doing well, they're preparing product launches for the next few quarters that were initially scheduled to occur in 2025. This is seemingly due to the fact that the world of work, media, and commerce has begun to accelerate toward being fully digital. In other words, the pandemic sped up the time machine and demanded that the future of work start now. The last thing you need is to get caught off guard.

Twelve years ago, Microsoft was the only technology company in the S&P top five, with a $273 billion valuation—a distant third to then-undisputed leaders Exxon Mobil ($430 billion) and General Electric ($364 billion). Fast forward a little over a decade, and the old industrial giants not only have been dethroned but have seen their valuations shrink to a tiny fraction of what tech companies are now worth. Exxon Mobil's value in 2020 plummeted to $197 billion, and General Electric's to $63 billion. So, what exactly happened during this last decade, and what does it have to do with your professional future?

First, beginning in the 2010s, capital markets started experiencing a complete makeover, which has greatly contributed to tech domination today. The active exchange of goods and services in physical markets is being replaced by access to digital products, services, and cultural experiences hosted in the cloud. Economic value, first created in markets, is now almost exclusively generated in networks, with consumption transitioning from retail, shopping centers, and trade fairs to search engines, social media, consumer apps, e-commerce, streaming, and subscription service platforms. Whereas before 2010 companies wanted to maximize transactions, they now seek to maximize relationships and monetize people in ways that don't require direct product selling. In fact, profits and selling are "so yesterday." With the financial backing of very patient, deep-pocketed investors, tech companies' primary goals are to achieve obscene market share and user growth first, then worry about profitability later.

With the tectonic shift to a digitally based economy, technology not only rules how we find an edge but how we build financial security. When digitization and computer networks win over traditional industrial markets, software becomes the cornerstone of value creation. Then the only thing between you and a severance package is Jedi-level human and cognitive skills, traits that separate you from computerized automation and turn you into a powerful ally to its rise, as machines grow cheaper and more powerful.

To be victorious in the digital race, there are essentially two principles for you, a modern professional, to assimilate. First, make sure you're on the right side of Moore's Law, and second, equip yourself with a set of specific skills, education, and knowledge that make you a partner to technology, rather than a target of it. Then, master key competencies in five areas: 1) human connection (political, social, and emotional); 2) communication (written and oral); 3) thinking (creative, critical, and analytical); 4) leadership (persuasive and driven); and 5) technical know-how (expertise in a fast-growing industry or segment).

It sounds like a lot, and it is, but every successful person has been doing this since free-market economies were invented. The only difference now is the velocity of change and how networks, not markets, hold the cards.

In summary, there's no easy path, or hardly a different one, even for entrepreneurs, contractors, or autonomous professionals to cross the digital divide. However, gaining a basic understanding of the economic forces shaping today's world and a sense of direction is a great start. After all, every winning strategy requires you to identify your strengths and where to apply them. Using the Dream Career Canvas framework, *Mind Definition* presents clear-cut guidelines on what to do to become a world-class professional in the 2020s. But first, let's take a quick look at modern markets to clearly understand why this makes sense and why you need to do what I suggest you do here.

A NEW CAPITALISM

The historical foundations of capitalism are shaken. For more than two hundred years, consumer markets were a place for property exchange between buyers and sellers. Now, they are a place of access between platform/intellectual property owners and subscribers/users. Markets versus networks and ownership versus access are examples of the contrarian forces of the digital age. Fueled by the exponential growth of computer power and the rise of sophisticated algorithms and machine learning tools, never-ending automation and digitization are the leading factors of wealth generation in the 2020s for both organizations and people.

For centuries, societies and institutions existed in a simple model that defined mostly tangible ownership of property—land, buildings, machinery, money, inventory, patents—all operating within the physical limits of markets—regional, domestic, international. Then global-ization and information technologies changed the landscape of human relations, creating a system where property still exists but has become more intangible in nature and very limited in exchange. In other words, property gets used, shared, and accessed increasingly more often, but property ownership doesn't change hands, and its accumulation and economic exploitation becomes concentrated, not spread.

As a result, we buy a lot less and subscribe a lot more for access to information and content than at any other age in history. It is not a coincidence that today's largest com-panies are either digital platforms or businesses that derive their value from exclusive networks of users. Take Google, for example, a company that transformed itself into our leading source of information. Google processes over 5.8 billion search queries per day, and at some level, we're all connected to its platform for information, communication, or any practical, material, intellectual, or social need. New York University professor and author Scott Galloway reveals in his book, *The Four,* that one in every six Google search queries have never been made before. This means that in times of inflated distrust of institutions and government, no current entity has more credibility and trust in consumers' minds than Google.

Intellectual capital and proprietary software drive the new era. Market transactions give way to agreements that include outsourcing, leasing, subscription, and affiliation to social networks and sharing platforms. Traditional au-tomotive brands are accelerating full-throttle towards paid-for access models where people can drive a full menu of luxury cars with a monthly subscription. Mercedes-Benz

Collection, BOOK by Cadillac, Care by Volvo, and Access by BMW are some of the services giving access to a premium selection of fancy toys without the strains of ownership and associated costs.[3]

Simultaneously, economic power comes less from capital accumulation and more from intellectual property ownership—copyrights, distribution rights, branding—and control of communication and network infrastructure. What is Uber, if not a computerized platform connecting millions of users with service providers on an IP-based, protectable source code? At a recent point, without owning a single vehicle, Uber was the world's most valuable transportation company. Instead of cars, it has proprietary technology that enjoys the power of network effects, enabling it to be present in over two hundred markets.

In the digital age, products are often subsidized or offered for free in exchange for relationships that lead to data collection—the digital age's *real* currency. The old capitalist system had buyers and sellers; the new has suppliers and users, with users volunteering labor in exchange for access. Facebook, one of the world's largest media companies, leverages user-generated content to unlock billions of dollars in advertising without investing a penny in original content. Worse yet, without compensating users for their creations and monetization of their data. While free user content supplies Facebook with an endless stream of engaging stories, Netflix shells out over $17 billion a year to produce and license new shows.[4] Yet, Netflix is another behemoth digital platform built on a subscription-based model, under the sophisticated hood of a highly secret, artificially intelligent system with *another* protectable source code. Netflix's real value is not in the content of its library—most Netflix shows are temporarily licensed, and their lineup changes all the time. Instead, its value rests on the predictive analytics and artificial intelligence of proprietary software that knows what people want to watch and engage with more.

As a second significant aspect, the networked age marks a tipping point from industrial to cultural production. We now have leisure time and cultural experiences being more and more commodified, digitized, and sold as original content, something Hollywood mastered decades before the Internet. The net result is an exponential growth in the number and size of companies and studios mining and packaging all kinds of human experiences through movies, documentaries, and television shows for profit. Examples include shows about exotic (non-Western) cultures, food, and travel; comedy, history, finance, and political commentary; weirdness and sensationalism; and human experiences in simulated-for-play environments, including social media, virtual game rooms, funfests, and online community-based events.

From a career perspective, understanding, empathizing, and connecting with people is not only key in solving business problems, but one of the most valuable skill sets for modern professionals to master, especially as companies pivot away from the traditional transaction-based model to new relationship-building models. Overall, digital economy consumers demand less accumulation and more experiences, bringing a cultural change that requires a new set of qualities for working professionals to survive, namely the Dream Career Canvas set of competencies and skills in booming areas of specialization, such as finance, technology, engineering, design, marketing, sales, and management.

WHY YOU MUST MANAGE YOUR CAREER

While the digital economy grants access to information and affordable services that contribute to a higher quality of life, it also generates inequality. In general, consumers extract incredible utilitarian value out of networks—entertainment, information, email exchange, file sharing, storage, teleconferencing—but very little of its economic value is shared. As technology brings abundance, it also generates higher output with less input—raw materials, financial capital, and labor—which creates a favorable scenario for corporations to produce and earn more while employing fewer people and utilizing fewer resources. The unintended consequence: innovation and GDP are higher, while wages are flat. Between 1990 and 2018, median family income in the United States rose, on average, 20 percent. In contrast, housing and college costs rose 50 percent each, while healthcare costs increased 150 percent.[5]

From a historical perspective, since the beginning of capitalism, wage and productivity growth went hand in hand. In the last twenty-five years, however, productivity and corporate profits have soared while wages stagnated. At the same time, we have witnessed three groups of people reaping most of the digital age economic value: financial capital owners, intellectual capital owners, and working professionals with outlier-level skills in the arts, sports, science, finance, and technology sectors. Together, these groups form what we can call a class of superstars—mostly in banking, engineering, natural sciences, creative production, and designing.

As economic value creation changes, coming less from routinized labor and more from abstract thinking, the ways we thrive in a digital economy also change. The cost of distributing original work is zero, more consumer surplus is created, and more innovation and originality are rewarded. To illustrate, proprietary software applications, intellectual property ownership, YouTube channels, e-learning courses, Instagram influencer videos, to name a few, give their creators residual income not bounded by labor hours or physical constraints. Simply put, they generate income in their sleep. In exchange, traditional skills—clerical, admin-based, data entry, customer servicing, among others—have limited value when automation and outsourcing can easily replace them. As a result, you must master social, communication, and innovative thinking skills to remain relevant, as those form your bulletproof vest against the digital age bots.

At this point, we can establish that a disproportionate amount of the Internet's bounty goes to content creators, innovators, and subject-matter experts in fields that require highly skilled training and education. While technology, finance, and healthcare management are now some of the breeding grounds for today's highly skilled, highly compensated professionals, other workers are seeing their wages flatten in almost every other sector.

The 2020s set the stage for machine power, where robots fulfill previous human roles, and humans with specific skills and credentials become indispensable in their work with machines. In this age, professional safety comes from jobs that require individual insights, where workers must tap into their intellect, sociability, creativity, and problem-solving skills—all traits that are hard to reproduce in software. Likewise, the days are numbered for activities that don't require those things. As such, the new human job security will rely more on abstract thinking, communication, and connection at a higher level, under the defining rules of augmented intelligence, the future era of intense collaboration between highly skilled workers and artificial systems.

Although in business rule-binding, routinization, consistency, and predictable decision-making will remain relevant, those are now the attributes of robots and digital systems—immensely superior to and cheaper than humans in this type of work. Conversely, the reward for humans will come from imagination, empathy, and people skills—now the future attributes of superior world-class professionals.

Advancements in digital connectivity give us unparalleled access to data and information. But while information and data are plentiful, professional wisdom only comes from high-quality career experiences. Harold Geneen, the legendary CEO of ITT Corporation, once said, "In the business world, everyone is paid in two coins: cash and experience. Take the experience first; the cash will come later." The lesson for career professionals here is clear—be always on the lookout for formative career experiences, as they are your primary source of upward mobility and financial independence. The more action-based knowledge you bring, the higher your earning potential becomes.

Some questions to ponder: Are you learning anything of value that can accelerate your career in your given industry? Do you *really* know your strengths and where you can best apply them? Do you have the opportunity to be in front of decision-makers who somehow provide you with honest, blunt feedback about your performance? Do you have any leader in your organization genuinely concerned about your development? Have you listed companies that you consider a great fit for your ambitions?

These are excellent questions to start asking yourself as you establish a career roadmap, because they focus on the three must-haves of career acceleration: finding the right company, the right boss, and the right assignments. Yet, we must look at the Dream Career Canvas's five principles in more detail to help you answer these questions and set you up for success.

1

PEOPLE AND POLITICAL SKILLS

Entire libraries of life wisdom out there speak of hard work, dedication, and talent as practically the sole ingredients for success. These attributes are important, of course, and certainly don't hurt—but overall, they are highly overrated. In reality, prosperity in life is more about sociability and relationship skills, mainly because human-organized institutions are nothing but emotional units led and run by people.

In general, no one achieves anything significant in life without somebody else's buy-in—especially when that somebody else is in a position of power. This is especially true in business. Most decisions on personnel hiring, promotions, assignments, training, coaching, and mentoring come from the top. Somebody always has to say "yes" to you, to your ideas, to your persona. To get a lot more "yesses" in life, it's crucial to excel at two items: 1) understand human nature, and 2) learn how to build relationships based on trust and mutual respect.

While the average person cares about being liked, the person of excellence cares about being *trusted*. You can't build trust, let alone relationships, without mastering people and political skills. If there's an area where everyone pretty much needs a boost, it's in building relationships. So here are nine strategies to help you ace relationship-building and get what you want professionally.

THE NINE RELATIONSHIP-BUILDING STRATEGIES FOR THE WORKING LIFE

▬ ▬ ▬

1. Get the Right Role at the Right Firm

This is imperative. Find your best fit or die trying (hopefully you won't die, but seriously, do your absolute best to know yourself and find out sooner rather than later where you belong). *Being the right person at the right place at the right time is the basic rule of professional success. Without fit, you simply won't build the relationships you need to advance.* Know your environment, the skills, the knowledge, and the traits that make you unique. Otherwise, your Herculean efforts will invariably lead to mediocre results, and you'll be judged as the proverbial fish trying to climb a tree.

Wharton School Professor of Management Peter Cappelli summarizes the amplifying effects of fit in a recent article, "HR for Neophytes," where he criticizes the myth of the "A" player. Cappelli says, "Most people aren't innately good, average, or poor performers. The quality of their work depends in large part on context, including the systems and support around them."[6]

In sum, the environment and the team are everything. The same article reveals that hiring a star performer from a rival organization often ends up in failure. The performance can't be replicated without the exact supporting structure of the previous company. More than anything, outstanding work depends on being in the right job with the right boss and coworkers. It benefits from being surrounded by people whose values, temperaments, and natural abilities can be associated with a given industry or career track—features that somehow match or promote your capabilities.

Finding our natural strengths is sometimes challenging. How do we know until we try? Early career opportunities can be a training ground for self-discovery. However, after a few years, you must be able to accomplish three essential things: 1) build character under pressure; 2) know how to deal with workplace demands; and 3) find a way to stand out.

More importantly, figure out which environment, culture, and career choice promotes your best qualities, then target the right industries, companies, and geographic locations to live. Your lifestyle should significantly impact your career decisions. Defining the city where you want to live should take top consideration as well. To dive into examples local to the author, healthcare, aerospace-defense, media and entertainment, insurance, and higher education are some of the dominating industries in Southern California. Concurrently, high tech, venture capital, and investment banking have places in Northern California. With notable exceptions, your career path will likely dictate where you'll live for most of your adult life.

Another point of interest now is remote work. While the work-from-home environment promotes more flexibility than working in an office, companies are unlikely to change to a 100 percent virtual model. Historically, creative collaboration and innovative work were always turbocharged by live human interactions—and substantial evidence points to remote work as a big hindrance to career promotions over time, with stagnation being the tradeoff for flexibility.

A separate factor, which is sensitive enough that hardly anyone brings to the table, is that aside from exceptional, extraordinarily talented people, a person's cultural makeup, language, appearance, and even gender can also influence career outcome. It shouldn't, but it does. Among many examples, male engineers traditionally do well in technology and high-precision manufacturing, whereas in fashion, media, and publishing, women are more likely to excel, especially in the fields of public relations and communication.

The same goes for nationality. French companies on American soil usually have a French person at the helm and in many C-suite positions. So do German, British, and Chinese multinational companies operating internationally.

As much as you dwell on exceptions and examples of extraordinariness beating the odds, the underlying factor is that your birthplace or ethnicity can also position you more or less favorably within a specific industry or company.

Your goal is to be good at something and perceived as so in the eyes of others when it comes to career choices. Sometimes your background and personality help. When they don't, you'll have to compensate with outlier skills of another nature. While not every personal trait involving nationality or ethnicity may translate into a career opportunity, it's important to consider how it might. Because when cultural fit meets passion and talent, you don't just become unstoppable—you face a less arduous path to the top.

Beyond stereotypes, though, you must find a workplace that fits your personality and skills, then your lifestyle. Self-awareness is what will bring you to recognize these realities and help identify areas where you will personally excel.

However, time is of the essence, so the sooner you figure yourself out, the better.

2. Get a Sponsor

When most people think of a sponsor, they think of a senior leader mentoring an apprentice on strategic direction and guidance—and traditionally, that has always been the case. But a mentor can be anyone good at something you want to become good at, including a colleague, an acquaintance, or a peer. So, in essence, a mentor-mentee relationship can be established whenever a person, regardless of role, is willing to work with you on building skills or competencies.

Strategically, though, a mentor must be an insider, preferably someone two or more levels above you in the organizational chart. And what will they do for you? A good mentor will protect you politically and assign you, directly or indirectly, projects of good visibility and learning. He or she will give you exclusive access to the most exciting aspects of the core business. In exchange, the mentor will rely on your informal feedback from the trenches. For example, your mentor will want to know how the staff is taking on big initiatives and projects and how upper management can help create more engagement. But it's very important to note that this isn't a channel for gossiping or backbiting, as this symbiotic relationship relies on positive reinforcement and feedback. As much gaining a mentor is politically strategic, support from colleagues is also crucial, or you'll get sabotaged.

Three types of mentors exist, depending on the situation: a *coach* to improve your performance in an area; a *sponsor* to push your interests in the organization; and a *connector* to properly introduce you to key people and power groups.

Finding a good sponsor is challenging for many reasons. Depending on their career stage, senior leaders may not be interested in sponsoring a junior staffer, as they might fear the impression of favoritism. Additionally, if they are influential, chances are they're already mentoring others. Your approach is to figure out how to become a valuable source to upper management and find a sponsor. You might consider changing departments to establish a special mentor-mentee relationship. Remember, you're always competing internally for resources, including the privilege to work on the more visible, career-accelerating projects that have "promotion" written on them. Having a sponsor is key to helping you stand out and get that kind of exposure.

Five Ways to Leverage Mentorship Wisely

Beyond sponsorship, define why you need a mentor. Are you looking for long-term career guidance? Are you trying to assimilate into the company's culture? Are you preparing for a specific assignment—a sales pitch, a presentation, a report draft?

Choose someone you can relate to, not just an influential person. Look for people you like and respect, someone you aspire to become someday. If you don't see that person in your current organization, you might be in the wrong one (for you).

Overdeliver. In general, mentors are motivated by legacies. They want to pass on their knowledge to mentees who are driven and competent. In exchange, mentors expect mentees to be organized and focused. You might promise, "I'll compile a complete sales analysis of our last two quarters by next week." The good mentee will follow up three days later with, "I know it has only been three days, but I have some preliminary numbers to share with you."

Be mindful of your mentor's time. Mentors are busy. Prepare your topics in advance. Take notes and define clear goals for each meeting session. Keep emails short. Leave philosophical discussions for one-on-one meetings. When you submit materials for review, allow enough time for feedback before you follow up.

Be an energy donor, not a taker. Show enthusiasm, excitement, and gratitude for the person's time. Don't gossip or complain. Always show up in a good mood, fresh, inspired, and ready to rock.

3. Build Your Network

Most career advisors tell you about the value of a good network and the types of networks better suited to aid career advancement. As a rule of thumb, you first need a professional network of like-minded individuals inside your organization. This network of colleagues, supervisors, and peers form the backbone of your industry connections. It will become precious over time, more so when its members change jobs and advance their careers in companies that are part of the same industry.

A second network you'll likely build is personal, as you'll eventually socialize and participate in groups outside of work. Those include school, college, training programs, and community-based associations where you live. Personal networks have the power of exposing you to different industries and segments, sometimes getting you closer to experiences and situations you'll never encounter in your line of work. Some of those lessons are transferable, so you not only benefit by connecting and learning from personal networks, but you also become better at what you do by socializing regularly.

A basic premise of building a healthy personal network: surround yourself with ambitious, motivated, hardworking people. A classic business school lesson on this is: *don't be interesting, be interested.* Find opportunities to help others, ask questions, show interest in things they do. Most people want to brag and have their egos massaged. Building relationships, instead, is about connecting, empathizing, and sharing.

4. Push Your Interests

Hardly anyone fights for you unless your benefit promotes their interests. That is natural, and it's one reason why connections are more about other people than they are about you. You must realize that competition for career-accelerating projects is fierce. Most workers rely on formal HR processes for promotion. Instead, you must push your interests to gain the exposure and formative experiences you need. Only in this case is gossiping a good thing. The more connections you have across departments, the more you hear about upcoming projects, promotions, and management restructures. Use this information to anticipate potential challenges and jump at opportunities. You must be strategic and attentive. Having a sponsor usually pays off here too, as you now have an ally to promote and mutually benefit from your interests.

Three soul-searching questions that can set the stage for success, and that you can answer solely by being proactive:

- Are you continually trying to learn new things at work?
- Have you asked for a mentor inside your organization?
- Do you engage in additional tasks beyond what your role requires on paper?

Suppose you're not pushing the envelope with unique insights and initiatives beyond your role description. In that case, chances are your career is plateauing, and you now must adopt a career-accelerant mindset that includes pursuing your agenda more aggressively.

5. Praise People Often

Everyone wants to hear about how valuable they are. Praising people for their good work not only enhances camaraderie but also boosts team morale. Simultaneously, people will unconsciously welcome your presence and share loads of valuable information with you just because you care. Foolish people talk about themselves; smart people listen and interject on crucial points, usually to provide feedback, give credit, or show gratitude.

If you're wondering how to build support and connect with others, wonder no more. All you need to do is listen, keep a positive attitude, and be part of the solution. By the way, research shows that sincere flattery is never enough. It's surprising how rarely professionals, on average, praise colleagues at work. So, be an outlier on sincere, well-deserved flattery, and stand out.

6. Be Loyal

Trust is everything; once it erodes—*goodbye*. It's not rare to see companies preserve less than stellar workers if they're trustworthy. Conversely, no amount of brilliance withstands the blow of disloyalty. A typical scenario where I see people getting fired unfolds this way: The team discusses one approach in preparation for a cross-departmental meeting. During the meeting, the disloyal colleague either changes course, contradicts the boss, or worse, connivingly transfers responsibility for something he/she did wrong.

Your loyalty to *people*, in general, is more rewarded than blind loyalty to organizations. Keep that in mind. As you progress throughout your career, outside forces often shape the company's destiny, and you are likely to be impacted by the repercussions of those events—especially in the case of an organization or division folding. Keeping your loyalty at the individual level helps you pivot. We live in an age where most people's careers will probably outlive the very companies they work for. Relationships of trust and respect, therefore, transcend companies. Cultivate them wisely, and you'll always find unlocked doors for new beginnings.

7. Always Deliver

Promises are a dime a dozen, results are much less likely, and astonishing results are rare. Most have good intentions, but what separates people at the top from those in the middle is quality and consistency. Obstacles always transpose between intentions and goals, and only the fierce prevail at materializing intentions where the majority can't.

At most companies, average workers focus too much on processes and procedures and too little on the big picture. Middle-of-the-road people, as a result, don't invest enough time building relationships or even in the skills that lead to participation in high-value projects.

Research shows that organizational awareness—or political awareness—is a common trait among top performers. For instance, organizationally aware people not only get a clear sense of priorities and initiatives in a place, but they also get things done with their peers' and superiors' buy-in. Conversely, people who are not politically aware always create plans in a vacuum, pursuing counterproductive tasks not sanctioned by senior management. In the process, they lose support for even the most basic aspects of their work, eventually joining an outcast group of practically no return.

If you want to be politically savvy, know when to get out of the office. Self-absorbed, task-oriented employees are likely to fatally isolate themselves. Besides job roles where introspectiveness and detail orientation are norms, most people benefit from a broader scope and perspective. Work on results (always deliver), and use daily socializing, mentoring, and feedback to your favor.

8. Consistently Build Career Skills

Learning is a never-ending process. The more skills you build, the higher you climb in your organization and the bigger the responsibility and pressure placed upon you. If you possess a growth mindset, that's the bargain you'll have to deal with. Therefore, building and learning the required skills to match your natural career progression at each stage is key. There are typically three stages to everyone's career: 1) depending on others; 2) contributing through others; and 3) leading through vision and strategic thinking.

Most career promotions start with solid technical skills. Those who excel at specific core areas become responsible for managing teams, eventually moving to the executive level where they'll lead units or entire organizations.

At first, technical knowledge is one of the most marketable skills to trade. However, its importance diminishes over time. Eventually, the more important skills center around effective communication and leadership—traits you gain through experience. As a result, the quality of your experiences often dictates your career path—including occasional roadblocks if you don't manage them well.

Most people stuck in middle management lack the social skills to keep moving. Those are individuals who usually fail to connect politically, focusing on processes instead of people, doing little to invest in relationships. How to avoid such a fate? First, excel in a technical domain. Become a good salesman, engineer, financial analyst, marketer. Know the ins and outs of your trade. Study hard, read, and learn by observation. Get a mentor and use every tool at your disposal to expand your knowledge base.

Simultaneously, build internal and external alliances. Work hard to strengthen your networks. Consistently get involved in group projects. They will give you a good grasp of human nature—examples include how to read people and fine-tune your emotional intelligence. At this point, you'll probably gain valuable lessons about how you contribute to others as well. You may even discover new talents you don't think you have, or simply find areas where you'll need to improve.

In the end, it's a process. Know what you need. Find out how to gain and develop your skills. Experiment. Measure. Evaluate. Rinse and repeat.

9. Relate to People on a Personal Level

Use every opportunity to hear more about people and get to know them as individuals. This one is tricky; but if you can avoid, never eat by yourself. Use lunch as an excuse to get to know coworkers on a personal level. Frequently invite others for lunch or coffee. Back in the day, when most people smoked, social studies found strong correlations between workplace smoking and promotions. Smokers took more breaks and spent more time in casual conversation with peers and supervisors who were also smokers. That created the social bond for stronger work relationships to form. Most people drink coffee or tea. Everyone eats.

Want to connect with a stranger or acquaintance? Get an introduction to talk about work. If they're colleagues, find ways to know them on a personal level. Share cool, inoffensive things about yourself that make you unique. For instance, I'm an Elvis Presley fan, something odd for a guy of my generation. Over time, I made many friends at school and work because of this fun fact. Some people find it curious, others just funny or amusing. It doesn't matter. It's an easy conversation topic that rolls into a personal trademark for me. Every time I connect to someone I haven't seen or spoken to in years, invariably the first question is: "Man, do you still like Elvis?" Not just that, but when people spot any Elvis reference, they remember me—and yes, I was told this many times. Find out what people's Elvises are and show a minimum of interest. Then, define things that make you unique and leverage them.

QUALITY PROJECTS: THE HIDDEN SECRET TO SUCCESS

High-quality projects are the secret ingredient to career success and the exclusive prize of those who master relationship building. If you're a force of positivity and drive, others will naturally gravitate to your orbit, eventually granting you access to this secret ingredient. When that becomes the norm, you'll generate meaningful results through exclusive initiatives that will help you build your brand. Fix a lousy process, patch things up with a discontent client, harness a partnership with a key supplier, or do anything meaningful that translates into better financials, morale, or engagement level numbers, and you'll forge a reputation of excellence for yourself.

Senior leadership and HR want to partner with people who demonstrate high potential and thrive in fast-changing environments everywhere. As a yardstick, they look for infinite learners who don't shy away from stretch assignments, collaborators with an internal sponsor, and a string of successful projects—even if they are sometimes minor in scale—under their belts. When corporate leaders see that, they detect a hipo (high potential) candidate and do everything in their power to create the environment for that person to shine.

More Reasons to Become a Hipo

In every organization, about three to five percent of workers are considered high potentials. Even though most organizations guard those lists of preferred associates with their lives or pretend they don't exist, companies shower hipos with exclusive projects and a disproportionate number of resources. One *Harvard Business Review* (HBR) study reveals that 98 percent of companies researched purposely identify high potentials, whether they publicly acknowledge it or not.[7] Likewise, 93 percent of the companies polled promote hipos faster than any other cohort of intelligent, hardworking, trustworthy individuals.

Smart, engaged, and ambitious people are the real drivers of competitive advantage in a knowledge economy. But where until recently companies selected and groomed associates on verbal, logical, and critical thinking skills, they now seek growth potential, adaptability, and resilience as traits. Since the strategy of today might not be the strategy of tomorrow, the competing industry of today might not be the competing industry of tomorrow. The only constant is change, and companies want quick studies who can perform amid fast, volatile conditions.

Likewise, the best workers are invariably driven by a few common threads—mostly autonomy, mastery, and purpose. In other words, what high performers seek out in a workplace is the freedom to make their own decisions (they hate being micromanaged), the motivation to excel at something, and the opportunity to serve a cause larger than themselves.

Companies understand hipos crave access to interesting people and resources. As a result, the priority in a large-scale enterprise is to assign premium projects to high potentials—exclusive assignments that will keep them busy and excited while generating impactful results.

The same HBR research reveals that 71 percent of executives consider "stretch assignments" the single most significant contributor to the unleashing of their potential and the fast-tracking of their careers, followed by "job rotations" and "personal mentors," each with 49 percent of the responses. So, people *currently* in highly regarded, executive-level roles at elite companies point to the quality of projects and mentoring as two of their most leading personal success indicators. I wish those who believe in the "my work speaks for itself" mythology could embrace this valuable lesson.

Hipos in Action

Hipos outperform their peers consistently in various circumstances. In addition to achieving superior results, they display behaviors befitting the general organization's culture and values, becoming admired by superiors and peers alike in the process.

A growing trend among organizations is zero tolerance for disruptive superstars. In consequence, brilliant jerks don't make the cut to hipo anymore, as companies overall embrace cultures of teamwork, collaboration, and mutual respect. In the contemporary scenario, what behaviors are companies expecting to find in potential hipo candidates?

- Infinite learning: As ambiguity, volatility, and uncertainty dominate, companies need individuals who can learn new skills all the time. People who display high curiosity, who constantly push for new knowledge and experiences, usually fit the bill.
- Motivation: People who display an inner drive for excellence are apparent, even to the casual observer. Common traits include an unwavering commitment to targets, as well as the willingness to sacrifice and compromise for goals that benefit the organization.
- Grit: The unshakeable drive to pursue challenging goals, despite facing intense hardship and adversity. Simply put, the ability to not get discouraged during tough times.
- Insightfulness: The capacity to look at information with a critical lens and detect patterns that correlate with novel solutions.
- Engagement: The capacity to persuade others with charisma and enthusiasm, subsequently motivating others toward collectively beneficial outcomes.

- Ownership mentality: Willingness to step out of the comfort zone, and the maturity to embrace stretch and other difficult assignments.
- Organizational awareness: Ability to read between the lines. A good sense of timing and opportunity.

How Can You Become a Hipo?

The basic formula to join the five percent starts with re-markable results. Then it moves to alignment, behavior, and leadership capacity, regardless of title.

Companies expect hipos to move from value creators to game changers. It's not enough to be intelligent; one must be wise. People that are too opinionated, who think they have all the answers, are brushed aside. Therefore, build your credibility. As your career progresses, technical skills make way for big-picture thinking and influencing.

Your performance gets you noticed; your behavior keeps you growing. Membership in the hipo list virtually transitions from "fit and affiliation" to "role model and teacher." More than that, you bring infinite learning with achievements. Too many people enjoy learning but put zero effort into implementing what they absorb. New knowledge must translate into productive action. As you do so, you build blocks for a hipo tracking with tangible results.

What else are you doing? You're learning and growing amid change and complexity. You're living and breathing your company's culture and values on a solid fifty-hour workweek. You're projecting a positive, non-threatening attitude that helps you earn company—and later, industry-wide—trust and admiration.

MANAGING UP

The most crucial working relationship to build is with your boss. Getting the right assignments and a good boss is just the beginning. Once you've achieved that, you must nurture the partnership—and that means exceeding your boss's expectations. For that, here are some of the things upper management expects from you but doesn't often vocalize.

Hard Work

Trending concepts of hard work are fleeting. Hard work means different things to different people at different times. However, at the very least it means working diligently to accomplish meaningful organizational goals, and typically logging more hours than the average person. Brilliant careers are hardly built on nine-to-five schedules. The concept of work-life balance has been greatly exaggerated in the last few years. The reality is that most meaningful things in life require considerable trade-offs, and often your personal life needs to come in second to whatever your job goals demand.

The overall goal is to avoid being the disengaged nine-to-fiver who complains about not having new opportunities for growth—the same person who doesn't invest in cultivating relationships with coworkers and remotely delivers Oscar-winning performances. The most basic approach is to start early and leave later. In large cities, where commute and traffic are issues, that's a strategy that helps you clear your head. It eliminates some of the stress of being stuck in traffic or arriving late. Nothing gives you more tranquility than getting to work before the rest of the group.

Conversely, some folks seek alternative hours to beat traffic on the way back by leaving mid-afternoon. Those are just more attuned versions of nine-to-fivers, as they often lack the vision to use the extra time for productive work.

Proactivity

Being inherently motivated and proactive about one's work almost always pays off handsomely. Most people's mottos are, "Tell me what to do, and I'll get it done." This sometimes translates to, "I'll pretend to get it done," but that's another story.

We're in the age of cross-functioning teams and flatter organizational charts, where qualities of self-management and self-regulation take a commanding role in the process of scoring points with upper management.

The general guideline: have initiative and think for yourself. Ask more questions about outcomes and strategic goals and less about procedures and how-tos. Unless they are babysitters or insecure micromanagers, bosses expect you to figure out the means by yourself while they happily share the envisioned outcome.

Intelligence

No genius is necessary. But doing more than simply asking "What do I do next?" all the time will take you a long way. Building powers of observation is critical in navigating the complexities of corporate structure.

Emotional intelligence, superior communication, and relationship-building skills comprise the sort of intelligence you should master. More than IQ (intelligence quotient), you must build PQ (political quotient) and EQ (emotional quotient) to stand out. Granted, some of that is built over time and with practice, but you can also improve tenfold by simply observing great players in action.

Reliability

To gain trust, you must consistently bring results. Another way to see this is by using the analogy of a checking account. Every relationship is a ledger, with debit and credit entries. Every good deed you make is a deposit into the relationship account with that individual. In contrast, favors or even apologies after taking misguided actions are withdrawals. Make sure you have enough balance before you attempt to spend that money. Most people start asking for things when they have zero credit and often end up to their necks in overdraft fees.

Ambition

It's common knowledge that high ambition people achieve more than low ambition people—and bosses know it. Although ambition often carries a connotation of greed, no successful person on Earth makes something of themselves without a healthy dose of ambition. Practical advice: treat ambition as your energy booster. Show that you're interested and share some of your long-term goals. If you're working for the right boss and at the right company (for you), then chances are they'll gladly throw you challenging, intellectually engaging projects to carry.

NAVIGATING TEAMWORK: THE ESSENTIALS

The most common element of a top-performing company is high-quality teams. World-class consultants often say companies are nothing but the sum of hundreds or thousands of conversations in a day—the better the conversations, the better the company. Yet, companies can't buy intelligent conversations or healthy interactions. They must develop them. As a result, solid, high-performing teams are rare, and it's obvious when you see one in action. If you want to stand out with career-accelerating projects, learn the ropes of fostering great teamwork. Here are some essentials to keep in mind.

- Most people want simple things at work, starting with meaning and a sense of belonging. That makes them operate with gratitude, creativity, and pride. Find a way to look at the big picture and share with teammates how their work fits within larger goals. Celebrate small victories and show gratitude for the contributions of others.
- Promote open communication. Don't be afraid to show vulnerability—people relate to those who are less than perfect. Trust only happens when people

allow themselves to be vulnerable in front of the team. When vulnerabilities are not present, a false sense of connection sets in—then, meaningful discussions never occur due to excessive political correctness.

- Know the difference between constructive conflict (ideological differences) and corrosive conflict (politics, ego, and mean-spiritedness). Never engage with the latter.

- Understand that most people only want their ideas to be heard and understood, even if not adopted. Allow them to share and debate on the merits of their thoughts.

- Always seek clarification at the end of meetings: "What have we decided today? Does anyone care to recap?" "From what I understood, this is what we agree to do . . ."

- Know that commitments rest on communication clarity and decision buy-in, not necessarily on consensus.

- Be attuned to office politics, culture, hierarchy, time pressures, and cross-departmental conflicts. Be a source of reason and self-control. Mediate, compromise, fanatically search for common ground. Focus on results and mutual benefits. Avoid rigid, insensitive postures or ideologies.

CARVING A NICHE IN THE COMPANY'S BIG PICTURE

There is danger in being so busy doing the job that you lose sight of your path. To craft meaningful work relationships and earn the golden ticket to the Charlie's chocolate factory of projects, ask yourself, "What is my organization's most important goal right now? Where is my industry going?" Compare the answers with the primary objectives of your division. Now you have a clue about what makes you relevant at the organizational level and what to be involved in for experiential learning.

Successful people divorce themselves from processes and marry results; they rarely focus on things they can't control. With that in mind, avoid lazy and incompetent team members; surround yourself with winners, like-minded people with proactive career approaches who don't whine or make excuses. Career success is not about being right all the time. Rather, it's about being consistently right a lot of the time. That requires you to work with a talented team.

In any profession, success hinges on the ability to manage yourself and your projects first, then others. Lead, motivate, engage. Develop superior emotional intelligence and self-awareness; know your character inside out—strengths, weaknesses, feelings, motives, and desires. If you don't have a cheat sheet, it's time to get one with the following questions answered:

- What are my strengths and weaknesses?
- What are my career or academic accomplishments?

- What's my biggest goal in life, and what am I working for?
- How do I respond to stress and conflict?
- What's my communication style—Driver, Analytical, Amiable, or Expressive? (See Part 2: Communication.)
- What are the communication styles of my boss and peers?

Suggestion: Take note of five behavioral traits that are hindering your climb up the corporate ladder. Examples are, "I have a hard time saying no," "I always express frustration when stressed," "I let negative thoughts and emotions get the best of me under pressure," and "I'm a perfectionist who often fails to meet deadlines because I seek perfection instead of workable solutions." Write them on a piece of paper and carry it in your pocket. Focus on one area of change per week. Do this until you reach an established outcome. Then switch to a new list. Repeat the process.

FOCUS ON THINGS YOU CAN CONTROL AND THINGS THAT HAVE AN IMPACT

Two life-changing questions everyone should be asking their bosses at the beginning of every working relationship or assignment are: "What do you want to be congratulating me on in my first six-month review?" and "What does success look like around here?" I bet millions of people out there are entirely oblivious to this, working aimlessly at things they'll never get measured on.

Other top priorities when starting a job or working assignment: Know who's who in the organization and what every person is responsible for; know who the sources of power are and who influences decision-making. Identify top Key Performance Indicators (KPIs) and what moves the needle on expected results. Other ways to build momentum and start creating Oscar-winning performances include the following:

- Always make your boss shine.
- Elevate others.
- Keep a positive attitude.
- Deliver on promises with results.
- Find ways to be in front of senior leaders to present unique findings/insights.
- Talk about your valuable work whenever possible.
- Join inside groups, volunteer, get involved.
- Even if you are the smartest person in the room, don't show, especially if you're a leader—let others shine and credit your good ideas to the team (senior management always finds a way to identify the sources of good ideas anyways). Everyone likes to feel they're contributing.
- Push for roles and opportunities you want. Don't take everything graciously just to please. It *will* derail you eventually.
- Look people in the eye and tell them they're essential to the team and the organization. Deep human connections are based on emotion, not logic.

- Don't worry about having all the answers. Look for questions that spark quality dialogues. When giving answers, buy time and listen to as many people and perspectives as you can before settling on a course.
- Devote your initial years to learning foundational skills in your area while building your networks, inside and outside the company.
- Early winning moves you faster. Build the most professional, political, and social capital from the start—always demonstrate drive, positive attitude, good listening skills, insightfulness, curiosity.
- Not everything you do is imbued with deep meaning—a lot of critical things in business are trivial, if not dull. You still have to do them.
- Carry GRIT—guts, resilience, initiative, and tenacity—as a badge of honor.

Luck and randomness exist. People get a lucky break here and there, and unfolding events create massive headwinds even for GOAT performers. But at least 80 percent of the results you'll get in life depend solely on mastering great principles and taking control of your career. At the end of the day, you're the only person who can manage how others perceive you. That includes the assessment of your results and the quality of your contributions. Always remember that reputations are built one conversation, one interaction at a time. Demonstrate resilience, posture, and positivity, and you'll be much closer to creating meaningful relationships at work.

2

PART

COMMUNICATION

More than information exchange, communication is about connecting and influencing. A HBR study points to effective communication as the number one factor accounting for workplace promotions in the United States today.[8] Along with leadership, communication is arguably the most popular contemporary theme in business education. Yet, most people fail to grasp its fundamentals, including talented professionals. Why? Because communication is more doing than knowing. To make it work, communication demands *years* of practice, commitment, and energy, plus solid self-awareness, knowing who you are, your abilities, your emotions; and then solid social awareness, knowing who people are, their abilities, their emotions.

On a basic level, the career world expects professionals to deploy good communication mechanics with strong written and verbal skills. The best advice on that is to pull a Picasso. He once said, "Good artists borrow, great artists steal." Watch strong communicators closely; observe their written reports, emails, and presentations. Look at how they express themselves in meetings, and analyze the way they talk to superiors, colleagues, and clients. Ideally, you'll find a way to establish a mentor-mentee relationship with communicators you admire, and you'll learn to mirror their ways over time.

In the meantime, however, it is important to consider the four personalities of communication.

THE FOUR PERSONALITIES
OF COMMUNICATION

The study of psychology dates to Ancient Greece when Hippocrates (460 BC–370 BC) identified four groups based on inherent temperaments and default communication styles. The four profiles here are derived from the original concept, later elaborated into a psychology model by Roger H. Reid and Denver University professor Dr. David W. Merrill, published in their book *Personal Styles & Effective Performance.*

1. Driver: a high–risk taker who wants to control and achieve. Works fast and alone. Administers the project and the group.
2. Analytical: a non–risk taker who wants to be right, a stickler for procedures and rules. Works carefully and alone. Keeps checks and balances.
3. Amiable: a non–risk taker who seeks harmony in relationships. A caring personality who is an integral part of a team. Keeps people getting along.
4. Expressive: a high–risk taker who is talkative, charismatic, and energetic. Exciting member of a team. Breaks the ice.

Most senior leaders are Drivers. So, it's important to consider how to effectively communicate with one.

- Be factual, efficient, and precise.
- Argue about facts, not feelings.

- Come up with a series of options and allow the Driver to choose between them.
- Ask: "What do you *think* about this?"

How to talk to an Analytical? (most mid-level managers, engineers, information technology [IT] professionals, compliance professionals, and business analysts are Analyticals)

- Give tons of data.
- Create a well-organized presentation.
- Offer choices supported by data.
- Ask: "What do you *think* about this?"

HR professionals, professors, counselors, and customer relations workers are typically Amiables. Now, how should one go about communicating with them?

- Be friendly, open, and agreeable.
- Don't offer a choice; offer incentives.
- Provide personal reassurances, such as: "I'll take care of it personally."
- Ask: "How do you *feel* about this?"

Expressives do well outside of tech-driven or detail-oriented work and are often found in sales. Now, what's the best way to speak to them?

- Give a fast-moving, enthusiastic presentation.
- Appeal to dreams and intuition.
- Show interest in things they are interested in.
- Ask: "How do you *feel* about this"?

Some performance-boosting behaviors to adopt, depending on which temperament is your default:

- If you're a Driver, exercise patience when others express themselves. Listen to what they are saying and try to understand their perspective before you speak.
- If you're an Analytical, be willing to take shortcuts and make intuition-based decisions every now and again. Try to respond more quickly when working with Drivers.
- If you're an Amiable, speak firmly and with assurance about your ideas and issues. Express a sense of urgency when appropriate.
- If you're an Expressive, keep emotions open but under control. Pay attention to the details of what others are saying.

THE ROLE OF EMOTIONAL INTELLIGENCE IN COMMUNICATION

Many things get in the way of effective communication. Noise, distractions, emotional and cultural barriers are some of the most common. However, from all the typical barriers or triggers, emotions are by far the most influential. When misused or not properly controlled, emotions thwart even the most knowledgeable professionals and the most artful storytellers. Conversely, when clearly understood and reined in, emotions spark superior human interactions instead, setting the stage for excellent working relationships to form. Thus comes emotional intelligence, the practice that helps you understand and manage your emotions.

Decades of behavioral research in human relations conclude that social skills are a better performance indicator than cognitive intelligence. Consequently, people study emotional intelligence to improve their interpersonal communication and build stronger social ties, where it's widely believed that until you develop what is called a strong emotional quotient (EQ), you'll continue to fail in advancing your career, regardless of how talented, educated, or bright you may be.

For most of the twentieth century, academics in professional sciences believed intelligence quotient (IQ) was the main predictor of success for work and school. After all, it was only natural to assume more intelligent people were more likely to succeed. But during the 1970s, a new powerful wave of behavioral research pointed to another direction, one that forever changed the understanding of how intellect and emotion contribute to greatness. This new wave revealed, among other things, that *people with high IQs in a work setting outperformed people with average IQs about 20 percent of the time, while people with average IQs but high EQs outperformed people with high IQs 70 percent of the time.*[9] Put differently, being emotionally intelligent was far better than being intellectually intelligent when it came to performance.

The same studies also found that while the intelligence quotient was fixed and genetically predetermined, the emotional quotient was flexible and prone to enhancement. For instance, 80 percent of the human brain develops from birth to age five, where children form their personalities and cognitive capacity for life. In other words, EQ is not only superior in predicting professional success, but it's also more feasible to develop, as one may become wiser and emotionally experienced with time, but not more intelligent in terms of IQ.

At this point, with almost fifty years of psychology research demonstrating the transformative power of the EQ, why is it that only elite performers deliver on superior communication and collaboration? The answer, ironically, is biological. While we are expected to use common sense, our bodies are naturally programmed to act quickly on emotions before reasoning. So, it takes a conscious effort to act with circumspection in response to emotion, and without proper management and control, our emotions hijack our behaviors. The ability to manage emotions and disallow them from hijacking our behaviors correlates directly with a high EQ.

A high EQ provides you with an immeasurable advantage for life. Researchers reveal that, on average, only 36 percent of people are good at spotting and understanding explicit manifestations of emotions.[10] And although we enter the workforce knowing how to communicate and perform relatively well, much of our career outcome rests on managing our profiles and channeling emotions for productive teamwork. To illustrate, here's an example of the elevator concept by Larry Senn, a celebrated corporate consultant. In his book *The Mood Elevator*, Senn indicates people are more productive when operating within higher emotional states, in a zone where they create the ideal platform for abilities to flourish.[11] The following graph is a simplified depiction of his theory. Looking at it, can you honestly say where you reside most days on the emotional spectrum?

Emotional States

The Penthouse

Higher Emotional States

- Creative, innovative
- Grateful
- Wise, insightful
- Resourceful
- Hopeful, optimistic
- Appreciative, compassionate
- Patient, understanding
- Humorous
- Flexible, adaptive, cooperative
- Curious, interested

The Basement

Lower Emotional States

- Defensive, insecure
- Impatient, frustrated
- Irritated, bothered
- Worried, anxious
- Judgmental, blaming
- Self-righteous
- Stressed, burned-out
- Depressed
- Angry, hostile

Emotional Intelligence in Action

As we assimilate the importance of spotting and managing our emotions, how can we develop strong enough EQ skills to communicate within the penthouse limits? The first step is to develop self-awareness. When you're self-aware, you understand the sources of your faulty behaviors. You spot negative feelings and thoughts before they surface, so you don't allow them to creep into your language. At the same time, you're looking for situations to demonstrate positivity and control. For instance, when you're self-aware, you:

- Remain cool, calm, and confident in every situation.
- Take time assessing the problem before you say or do anything.
- Carry a positive outlook with an orientation toward action.
- Project compassionate kindness, even when you disagree.
- Demonstrate patience and understanding during stressful situations.
- Respect different points of view.
- Refrain from taking things personally.
- Work well with people of different personalities.

The second step is to develop social awareness. When you operate with social awareness, you read others' emotions and understand what triggers certain behaviors in your peers. When you're socially aware, you know the big picture while you do the following:

- Capture the emotions in the room

- Say the right thing, at the right time, with the right tone (confident, empathetic, respectful, assertive)
- Put yourself in other people's shoes
- Build relationships based on shared goals rather than personal views of the world
- Share opinions with poise, security, and emotional control
- Never lose an opportunity to make others feel smart and confident

Communication skills essentially make or break careers. As globalization and technology outstrip organizational charts of mid-level positions, companies keep high performers at the forefront while outsourcing or automating average ones. Being a higher performer today means having the ability to display higher EQ levels. Combined with proper technical skills, EQ makes of you one asset companies can't afford to lose.

NOISE: THE GREATEST VILLAIN IN COMMUNICATION

Communicators compete with all kinds of noise. The average person is bombarded with 35,000 messages a day, including emails, texts, billboards, broadcast, and social media.[12] But while information overload interferes, noise in communication mostly stems from differences in biases, perceptions, and emotional states among people.

As a rule of communication, the full responsibility to get the message transmitted belongs to the sender. The sender is 100 percent responsible for not just getting the message across, but ensuring the message is understood. In short, good communicators don't worry about being clear—they worry about being understood. They understand effective communication is rare because people operate by different mental models and communicating styles, and in response, good communicators master the art of identifying and responding to those differences. Based on this approach, you can also deploy a few noise-breaking tactics: Assess the communication styles of those around you. Understand what makes a Driver or an Analytical tick. Adapt your delivery to engage with Amiable or Expressive team members. Define the benefit of what you're saying by who's listening. Frame the idea from your audience's perspective. Remember, communication is conscious. You can always choose how you communicate.

THE POWER OF LISTENING

Social studies suggest listening skills account for roughly 40 percent of total information exchange.[13] And while more passive than speaking in general, listening is a complex task. The usual suspects—noise, stress, pressure—make it a lot harder than it seems to listen effectively. Nonetheless, being a good listener is paramount to empathetic communication and career progress. So, here's a small sample of behaviors you typically see most good listeners displaying.

- They acknowledge the speaker.
- They boost the speaker's confidence and self-esteem.

- They monitor their body language, silently signaling to the speaker that he or she is important and not being judged.
- They invest in conversations that spark trust and cooperation.
- They're genuinely curious about what others have to say and how they feel.

Now, let's talk about things to say. When listening, keep any interjections open-ended and considerate. Your interjections should encourage further conversation instead of shutting it down, and take the discussion one step further. Here are some examples.

- "I see."
- "I understand."
- "That's a good point."
- "Tell me more."
- "Help me understand this better."
- "Say more about that."
- "Please continue."
- "Then what happened?"

Other approaches by which you will gain valuable input from one-on-one communication include the following:

- "What alternatives do you see?"
- "What do you propose?"
- "How can we make it better?"

In contrast, poor listeners miss out on valuable cues and squander opportunities to build trust. Poor listening might be characterized by the following behaviors:

- Constantly interrupt.
- Make limited eye contact, get easily distracted, or suggest the speaker doesn't have the listener's full attention.
- Jump to conclusions about the speaker's message that are often incorrect.
- Change topics in the middle of the conversation.
- Take too many notes and don't tune in to body language.
- Demonstrate impatience or annoyance (yawning, eye-rolling, staring at the floor).

If you're wondering where you stand, here's a personal checklist to see how you behave during conversations.

- Do I listen to understand, or do I spend most of the time mentally preparing for my next remark?
- Before jumping to respond, do I reflect and make sure I understand what others mean?
- Do I summarize points of agreement and disagreement to engage in discussions?
- Do I show sensitivity and respect when I emulate a contrarian point of view, observation, or criticism?

THE ART OF CONNECTING

The average person speaks about 16,000 words per day, enough to fill 300 pages a week if transcribed.[14] But talking and connecting are two different things. In most organizations, there are too many people talking and very few connecting. This results in a lot of important discussion falling on deaf ears, ideas that aren't fully formed or deeply considered, and requests that don't trigger action. To avoid this, you must change from a person who's talking to a person who's connecting. When connecting, you are doing the following:

- Projecting focus on others; displaying a warm, positive attitude
- Using gestures, stories, and analogies to convey meaning
- Spotting opportunities for common ground
- Being authentic, entertaining, funny, inspirational
- Speaking with simplicity—getting straight to the point
- Celebrating people's successes
- Giving credit for good ideas
- Asking meaningful questions
- Smiling; projecting radiant energy

Great connectors bring people together; they're the glue for groups to form. They talk substantially more about others than themselves. Before a meeting, they show up with back-pocket questions. They talk with others instead of talking at them, while their radars are tuned to desires, fears, and anxieties; they are always searching for a common ground on which to bond. In short, connection requires outward focus.

Celebrated author and leadership guru John Maxwell brings specific insights about connecting in his bestselling book, *Everyone Communicates, Few Connect.* In this work, Maxwell suggests talking about your successes if you want to impress but speaking of your failures if you're going to connect. He also cites the impact of attitude in creating great first impressions, especially with body language. In Maxwell's view, you are the message. To illustrate, he invites readers to ask themselves whether they walk with energy and confidence rather than being hunched and distracted. Ultimately, Maxwell believes connection failure is a by-product of immaturity, afflicting those who insert themselves at the center of everything. It's his belief that one of the earliest signs of professional maturity is the realization that achievements in life are not just about you or your desires. To connect, you must act on behalf of others. Only then will your goals advance.

THE ART OF PERSUADING

The most successful people in every field are the ones most talented at persuasion. In the United States, economists attribute 25 percent of today's employee compensation levels solely on persuasive qualities.[15]

In his book *Changing Minds,* Harvard University professor and developmental psychologist Howard Gardner characterizes great persuaders as artful storytellers. Their media and approaches vary—leaders may persuade with stories, while scholars and scientists may use theories, and artists with creative expression—but they *all* project authenticity. Examples of how persuasiveness in communication works in business and life include:

- Entrepreneurs persuade investors to finance their start-ups.
- Job seekers persuade hiring managers to offer access to professional opportunities.
- Politicians persuade voters to come to the ballot.
- Leaders persuade employees to generate results.
- CEOs persuade analysts to rate their companies favorably to protect stock prices.
- Sales professionals persuade consumers to choose their products.

Persuasive communication is a survival skill. Warren Buffet, the legendary investor and Columbia University graduate, holds persuasion so dear that the only diploma he frames in his office is a Dale Carnegie public speaking certificate he earned in the 1940s.[16] Simultaneously, Buffet often tells students in his public speaking events that communication can boost their professional value by 50 percent instantaneously—now, consider this over the course of a career.

Scientific studies indicate that powerful storytelling and persuasive communication trigger the production of oxytocin—the hormone and neurotransmitter responsible for bonding. Presenting research on the 500 most successful TED Talks of all time, *The Wall Street Journal's* best-selling author and speaker Carmine Gallo reveals the following: highly-rated presentations, on average, are made of 65 percent stories, 25 percent reasoning—facts, figures, relevant information—and 10 percent character, who the speaker is and what he or she represents.

Today's world is so full of average, uninteresting, and disengaged people that a passionate storyteller stands out. Some of their qualities are easy to spot. Author and communication expert consultant Sonya Hamlin contrasts excellent and average communicators' attributes in her book, *How to Talk So People Listen*. For instance, she points to great speakers as warm, friendly, knowledgeable, organized, creative, confident, inspiring, authentic, and funny. Conversely, middle-of-the-road speakers are often pompous, vague, flat, complex, patronizing, stuffy, formal, and monotonous. When it boils down to connection, those projected qualities make all the difference.

In Ancient Greece, while elites used rhetoric to manipulate people, they didn't want the secrets of storytelling shared. Aristotle was not one of them. The great philosopher fervently believed in storytelling as a transformative tool for all. In his magnum opus, *Rhetoric,* the foundational treatise of persuasion, he laid out the three components of influence: *ethos, pathos,* and *logos. Ethos* is the orator's credibility and appeal; *pathos* is his emotional connection with the audience; and *logos* is his logical reasoning. With this premise, Aristotle single-handedly established rhetoric as an art form, inspiring entire generations of leaders in communication. It's no surprise we still talk about his legacy today.

While Ancient Greece may or may not have many parallels with our age, it certainly has one in persuasion. Now as then, human enterprise still demands knowledge sharing and storytelling to function. Individuals who can't do that suffer.

3

PART

ORIGINAL
THINKING

Innovation is the engine of the knowledge economy, and it is fueled by original thinking—the capacity to absorb information, assess value, and deliver on-point insights about facts or situations. Regardless of what you do, you'll need sound judgment and a great mix of book and street smarts to produce original thinking and get to the top professionally.

There are three attributes of original thought: critical, innovative, and analytical—or what I call "CIA thinking." Deployed in different situations, all three help superior professionals navigate career and life complexities. Let's see critical, innovative, and analytical thinking in action, along with some strategies for you to master them.

CRITICAL THINKING

This is the established process of reflection, reading, pondering, and observing. For instance, do you believe everything you read? Do you ever question the underlying motives of people you hear or listen to? Do you make assumptions on out-of-context information?

Critical thinking, in other words, is the art of assessing value in people, things, and situations. It's a tool to objectively evaluate your strengths and weaknesses, plus the opportunities and risks life throws at you.

Generally, the bigger your scope and perspective on history, human psychology, current political, socio-economic, and technological events, the more equipped you are to make well-informed decisions. Once you realize critical thinking requires you to continually seek quality information and knowledge, you treat it as a hygiene factor. You shower every day, and the benefits will be self-evident.

Operationally, critical thinking helps you manage time and resources by defining what you need to do first, whose buy-in you need to obtain, and what activities impact your goals. Professionals who exercise critical thinking read and interpret instructions well, understand hidden motives, and separate essential information from noise. In contrast, professionals who lack critical thinking often get manipulated or bypassed for growth.

Critical thinking is one of the most vital aptitudes to have in life, not just to operate as part of an organization but to manage a career. It's dangerous to be so busy doing your job that you forget to look up and see where you career is heading. Good critical thinking skills keep you grounded. With them, you know exactly who you are and where you're going at all times.

While we can always allocate a small portion to randomness, at least two-thirds of professional success is controllable. So, in addition to studying, training, and staying well informed, how do you leverage critical thinking for career planning?

- Broaden your scope. Understand what's happening globally—consider the best career tracks for your skills, the fastest-growing companies and industries to join, and trainings and experiences that are in high demand.
- Ask yourself, "How much of my skill set is unique?" Getting into highly competitive fields may put you

in a race with very talented, credentialed people. If that's the case, how can you stand out?

Outside forces play a part in the types of head and tailwinds you'll encounter. Global competition, regional economy transformations, fiscal and monetary policy changes, societal trends in consumption, and more, are always lurking. Albeit challenging, they're still conquerable with the compass of critical thinking for guidance. Without it, they're lethal.

INNOVATIVE THINKING

Have you wondered where creative ideas come from? Some are quick to point to creativity as a natural trait. The sources of innovative thinking, though, are more nuanced than that. There's a degree of process and experimentation involved.

In a nutshell, everyone is creative or has the capacity to be so, but most people don't see themselves as such. In real life, striking gold in innovative thinking requires a lot of trial and error. Thus, it's easier to see creative solutions as an offspring of fertile, artistic minds and to completely ignore the grueling, invisible work behind them.

For business and career, the most chased innovations are designed to enhance the customer experience. Products in the digital economy are heavily subsidized, and almost everything is commoditized. What differentiates companies is their brand experience and unique storytelling—and guess what? The corporate sector handsomely rewards people who can help them ideate those differentiators.

Every business innovation presents trade-offs between what consumers want, what the technology permits from a technical standpoint, and what companies can afford financially. In the end, the perfect experience consumers envision is always limited by how much you can scale and deliver at a profit.

Several methodologies in business and academia have been launched to capture, bottle, and distribute creative thinking—in short, to accommodate the trade-offs that lead to breakthrough innovation. Perhaps nothing in corporate America has done more than design thinking to promote creative thinking at both individual and organizational levels. Although not perfect, the five stages of the design thinking framework—empathize, define, ideate, prototype, and test—democratize innovation and bring world-class industrial design principles to everyday professionals. Since popularized in the 1990s by Ideo, the Silicon Valley venture that, among other products, designed the original mouse for Apple's Lisa, millions of people have found in design thinking the inspiration to think and act creatively in the workplace.

Unless you're an outlier, unleashing your creativity and delivering innovative solutions does not imply you'll suddenly create life-changing things at work. It simply means that 1) you should believe you can bring original solutions for most problems, and 2) you should learn how to operate with empathy. Design thinking emphasizes that empathy is the foundational element of innovative thinking. Once you start framing issues and situations with the unique perspective of others in mind, you're already a step closer to identifying better solutions to problems. Clever ways to improve your department's processes and design more engaging meetings are some creative initiative examples. Also, improving communication between departments A and B and reducing client inquiries by launching a self-service portal qualify as innovative, intrapreneurial practices.

Externally, however, most people approach empathy by mining customers' feedback to improve their experience and make more sales. Just like critical thinking, innovative thinking must be mapped out and practiced. The first step is to bypass the fear of rejection and to experiment with new ideas. A few strategies include the following:

- Build superior observational powers, spot behaviors, seek feedback.
- Start small. Propose a customer journey map creation with your team. Frame other groups as internal customers if you're in operations.
- Improve simple working processes as a quick way to gain confidence and experiment with small changes.
- Read more about design thinking. Consider taking affordable online workshops on the subject to get your creative juices flowing.

These strategies will give you insights to delight people and deliver more value to teams, bosses, and clients. Remember, innovation is a numbers game. Only multiple attempts lead to truly innovative ideas. But first, you must believe you can, then roll your sleeves up and try.

ANALYTICAL THINKING

Analytical thinking can be defined as a mix of training, education, and intuition to support evidence-based decision making. The Internet of Things, sensors, and other forms of big data technologies give companies powerful tools to collect and extract information that theoretically leads to making smarter decisions and achieving better results.

But this whole process is contingent on one's analytical ability. Finding solutions in business is a balance between being good at looking at hard data and at the same time relying on feeling, intuition, and sensorial perception. Combined, these powers of observation and deductive reasoning conduct what the language of business calls qualitative and quantitative analysis.

Analytical thinking is the prime competency of the modern workplace, mostly at a tactical level but also at a strategic corporate level. Every organization wants a worker who can interpret data by identifying cause-and-effect relationships, while also describing, prescribing, and predicting potential data-based outcomes.

In addition to interpreting accounting and financial statements, quantitative analysis in business requires understanding basic statistical models—such as sampling, percentages, regression, and ratios. Having the capacity to measure consumer response, engagement, and awareness levels, plus overall perceptions about brands, promotional campaigns, and value propositions are some of the most rewarded analytical competencies at enterprise level.

While many digital economy commentators today are quick to dismiss the value of higher education, this is the type of training most young professionals get exposed to in college first. So, whether you gain it from college or other types of study, a few strategies to excel at analytical thinking should include the following:

- Learning entry-level principles of statistics: means, middle and modes, standard deviations, regression analysis
- Studying Microsoft Excel tools: v-lookups, pivot tables, functions
- Reviewing elements of marketing research: survey design, focus group mediation, secondary data analysis
- Mastering workflow charts and decision-tree creation
- Understanding financial concepts: cost of capital, net present value, internal rate of return, discount rates

Luckily, these concepts are not rocket science, and you can find sufficient online training. So, even if you have been running from numbers your entire life, don't make excuses. Find what you need and become a professional who uses rational, evidence-based, data-driven thinking.

HOW TO BEAT AUTOMATION: THE ABOVE, ASIDE, AND AHEAD (AAA) PRINCIPLE

Watch out! Robots are coming for your job. How many times have you heard similar statements? Too often, probably. Most recent articles and books about technology and the future of jobs quote a 2013 study led by Oxford University researchers Carl Benedikt Frey and Michael A. Osborne called "The Future of Employment: How Susceptible are Jobs to Computerization?" The study estimates that about 47 percent of today's occupations in the United States are at a high risk of being automated within the decade, but mostly in logistics, transportation, and office support roles.[17]

Gaining skills to hedge against the next technological turn is always wise. We should never downplay the threat of automation in general, even if the analysis says job displacement will be more likely self-contained within three segments. Here's how our interpretation of the study differs from that coming from the "horsemen of the apocalypse" commentators out there. As machines and systems grow in precision, the value of high-level abstract thinking and human communication goes up in terms of creative collaboration and problem solving. Modern workers must then find ways to excel at human-centric skills. In fact, the study points to education attainment and creative and social skills as antidotes to the risk of job loss due to machine learning.

To put it simply, as the demand for educated, critical thinkers grows in the twenty-first century, so does the demand for human-centric, social, creative skills. And while the "sky is falling" argument that artificial systems will kill all the jobs is catchy, we should flip to a more realistic narrative: The real digital age challenge for humans is not to run against machines but to work well with machines. That means you don't have to worry about job displacement as long as you offer the sort of skills that complement the work of artificial systems while also being able to connect socially.

One of the paradoxes of employment is that companies want your experience—but leading companies expect you to find that *initial* experience someplace else. So, considering the two variables of 1) growing automation and 2) leading companies seeking ready-made skills, how do you safely compete for great jobs? The first lesson is to make sure you're on the right side of Moore's Law. The future holds a place for knowledge professionals to work with machines and create things that neither could do independently. When machines take over repetitive, routinized tasks, humans can spend a lot more time on higher value, more nuanced work. Even in today's automation-driven era, where intelligent systems take over some of the responsibility that was once delegated to a human being, machines cannot yet substitute for flexibility, judgment, and common sense. With that in mind, the AAAs are essentially three career approaches for augmentation you should pay special attention to for accelerated growth.

Stepping Aside of Technology

By "stepping aside," I mean moving out of the way of technology. Emerging digital age working groups benefit from building expertise in human-centric traits, such as context, narrative, synthesis, and emotional connection. Many professional roles require abstract thinking, artistic, or expressive human touch. Think of copywriters, designers, sales professionals, healthcare providers, and instructors. They operate in environments of spontaneity, sensibility, imagination, and improvisation. Despite remarkable advancements in computing power and machine learning, those areas are likely to remain fortresses for well-paying jobs since computers are way too far from operating in that capacity yet.

Besides, body language and physical expression in sports, arts, and fashion constitute another robust, human-dominated segment. Entire professional classes use their bodies as instruments to create, communicate, and relate to the world. Professional actors, dancers, models, musicians, elite athletes, and others benefit from stepping aside of technology, successfully leveraging their physical dexterity or aesthetic appeal for financial gain.

In sum, unless you picture a world where autonomous systems fully codify advertising, art, sports, and specialty services, stepping aside of technology will be an excellent robot buffer. As a takeaway, consider placing your chips in "stepping aside" careers if you're expressive, creative, or derive inspiring energy from social interactions.

Beyond the most visible jobs in pro-sports and arts, other stepping aside careers include graphic designer, brand manager, professor, visual artist, writer, composer, cinematographer, sales manager, diplomat, government official, politician, and lawyer, among many others.

Stepping Above Technology

Highly skilled and specialized knowledge has always created protective moats for professionals. Advanced degree holders make more money in general and experience a less bumpy ride in the job market than most workers in areas ranging from science and education to corporate leadership and consulting. In a sense, the wisdom of finding career security through higher education persists, and to some extent it is promoted by technology.

Forbes recently published a list of best and worst master's degrees for jobs based on research from the software company PayScale. Biomedical engineers ranked at the top, with a midcareer compensation level of $129,000 a year and highest job satisfaction among participants interviewed. Master's degrees in corporate finance, strategic management, and statistics also ranked higher on midcareer compensation and job satisfaction, signaling potential growth pathways for top money and career fulfillment.[18]

Researchers, analysts, and consultants are some of the professionals benefiting as part of "stepping above" strategies. If one of these professions fits into your plan, consider pursuing higher education and expertise equally transferable across fields—or, at the very least, hard to reproduce by software. Careers in big data, for instance, are up and coming today in research and corporate strategy. Leverage such training with pattern recognition and storytelling competencies, and you will position yourself for extremely lucrative jobs in professional services, marketing analytics, education, science, engineering, and applied mathematics areas.

Stepping Ahead of Technology

We have talked extensively about human-specific traits. What about machines? What are artificial systems truly capable of? Machines excel at codified, structured, repetitive tasks based on rules, parameters, and limits. Modern experts believe machines can make better decisions than 90 percent of the people in operational roles.[19]

Still, machine rules and parameters are human creations, so much so that many of today's most prestigious jobs are in segments defining the future of machine operation, including areas of artificial intelligence, virtual reality, and algorithmic creation designs.

Logically, a "stepping ahead" strategy gives a tremendous competitive advantage for talents capable of designing such systems. If that's you, technical skills in advanced software, robotics, mathematics, and computer science are mandatory. For instance, a business degree with IT-related expertise makes an incredible combo as you build analytical powers to detect where existing systems fall short.

As companies face hard-pressed regulation on data privacy and compliance issues, some career choices ahead of technology with incredible potential include hardware and software engineering, risk management, data systems architecture, cybersecurity, and audit related roles. Furthermore, degrees, certifications, or legitimate working experiences in those areas can help you build marketable skills that apply to every industry today.

NAVIGATING YOUR CAREER

We all start our careers developing ground-based technical skills. Then we generally keep moving by excelling at those skills until we hit a roadblock. That roadblock is middle management, where the skills that got us there won't get us any further.

Here's what usually happens. At the beginning, you learn a craft skill, become good at that, and get promoted. Now you're in charge of a department or division where the main goal is to get work done through others, and actually doing the work leads to failure. Think of a micromanager who wants to be a sole hero instead of a delegator, who's always burned out, and yet sees himself as extremely valuable for showing grit. Companies have plenty of those managers—too many, in fact. So, here's a rule for the newbie manager or supervisor who wants to do better than that: If you continue to perform the same tasks you always have, there won't be a reason for you to get promoted. Instead, build additional skills in time and workflow management, coaching, feedback, and performance analysis.

Once past the middle management hurdle, only a select few move to the top. In addition to making management, these top players make sure to acquire people and political skills when promoted to leadership. People skills serve to help them engage with direct reports, thus creating more cohesive teams. Similarly, political skills build political muscle with upper echelons, helping them compete with other managers for internal resources.

Being successful in middle management, therefore, is crucial for top money and long-term growth. Those who navigate this stage well often reach the top, where their skills in politics and influence developed in the middle now forge strategic thinking at the executive level. In short, midcareer level skills, which can be found nowhere else, offer senior leaders invaluable tools to set a vision, communicate, and mobilize.

The Four Stages of Competence.

In the 1970s, Noel Burch, then working for Thomas Gordon, the legendary clinical psychologist with leading works in business communication and conflict resolution, introduced the "Four Stages of Competence," a revolutionary training matrix for human learning. According to Burch, people go through the following four distinct stages until achieving mastery of a subject.

Stage 1: Unconscious Incompetence

People are unaware of their lack of knowledge, or what many call "innocent ignorance." At this stage, they don't know what they don't know, and the only way to move up professionally is by recognizing their ignorance about the knowledge, skills, and competencies they need to master. On a company level, individuals depend on others to contribute.

Stage 2: Conscious Incompetence

Here, individuals recognize how much they have yet to learn and master while looking for ways to close the knowledge gap to achieve their goals. In practical terms, conscious incompetence is the awakening to the realities individuals must learn. They start noticing top performers in their industry using skills and domains they barely understand. Most people give up at this stage, as the task of developing tacit knowledge and building expertise is daunting, sometimes taking years to complete without any tangible or immediate reward. On a company level, they start contributing *independently*.

Stage 3: Conscious Competence

Years of practice lead to the conscious competence stage. Here, people achieve above-average results with focus and determination, but hard work is still required. This is the stage where rewards are tangible, such as promotion, salary increases, or peer recognition. Anyone who gets to this point is likely to continue development towards subject mastery, having passed the stage at which most give up. On a company level, individuals are contributing *through others*.

Stage 4: Unconscious Competence

When it becomes an individual's second nature to excel at a task, suddenly it's not just something one does but something one becomes. Here, the results come effortlessly to the amazement of others. What most fail to recognize, though, is the grueling process leading up to the unconscious competence stage. On a company level, individuals are leading through *vision*.

How the Stages Apply to Career Management

At first, you're the novice, entirely unconscious of your ignorance and potential. When you first start in a company, you don't have the necessary knowledge to succeed yet. Often, you're even unaware of what knowledge you need. In this case, formal education's role is critical, especially for those not blessed with positive role models. Education not only has the power to stimulate your passion for a given subject, but it also gives you a clear sense of mission, something to consider devoting your life to accomplish. At a minimum, you should seek successful people to emulate and to learn valuable lessons from.

As you learn the ins and outs of the trade and get a grasp on the overall industry in terms of client, competition, and products, you then attune to the things you need to master to become successful in that field, characterizing your intermediate stage of conscious incompetence.

The third stage is of the skilled practitioner, or conscious competence. Individuals at this stage have probably moved into leading teams and bearing more responsibility. This is where your confidence starts to peak. And if you happen to align your work with inner values and a sense of mission, you're a strong contender for unconscious competence—the optimal stage of effortless brilliance that also leads to mentoring, teaching, and developing others.

Technical skills normally lead the way to your general career progress. Over time, most people master technical, company-based activities when engaged. Those who reach the top of their organizations invariably pair technical competencies with people and political competencies. Your toolkit, therefore, must include these.

External factors also play a role. In corporate America, many have written about Baby Boomers delaying retirement post-2008, vastly diminishing the opening slots for strong Generation X and Millennial candidates, especially in more traditional industries outside of technology and finance. HR professionals refer to this phenomenon as the "gray ceiling." The general advice is, again, to find sponsorship and support inside the organization. Somehow you need an influential person to vouch for you and get you on a path to promotion. Other alternatives are changing industries, moving to a different (probably smaller) company inside the same sector (more likely for most people), or simply tackling a difficult problem that keeps upper management awake at night—our celebrated "Oscar-winning performance." Those are all challenging moves—but hey, nobody said it was easy.

ULTIMATE CAREER ADVICE: STAY CLOSE TO THE PRODUCT OR THE MONEY

At every company, it is an unfortunate reality that a small subset of employees receive a lot more money, experience, and career progress value than everybody else. Typically, the people who are closest to product creation and sales are the ones who gain access to upward mobility in the corporate ladder while others lag in lower-rank, operational and administrative roles that are often underpaid and lead nowhere. Here's what nobody tells you outright: the people in top management, sales, or directly involved in product development reap almost all the rewards in most organizations. This is because creating a new product, finding new growth markets, and generating sales is more difficult than performing predictable and routinized administrative work, as much as those activities are crucial for the business's survival as well.

Therefore, anyone aiming at real career mobility must realize that this is how the game is played. In a company's eyes, everyone is valuable, and they can't demoralize people or lead anyone to believe the system is unbalanced. However, the underlying truth is more complicated than the corporate sugar-coated version, where, indeed, those who bring higher value get higher value in return.

You may see your valuable contributions in operations deserving more than the standard three to five percent merit increase, while upper management is just happy your activities didn't exceed projected costs. Their eyes are on the ball, and the ball primarily is in sales, more growth, and establishing new clients, products, and services. Everything else is a "cost of doing business," including your salary and that of your talented administrative team.

Thus, part of your career strategy is to build the skills to move up to the profit center side of the business, where exclusive opportunities for promotion and serious money-making reside. To put it simply, it's not that you don't bring value inside a cost center—it's just a lot harder to make a quantifiable impact for the business and prosper there. There's minimal recognition. The comparison below may help to illustrate this point.

Cost Center Definition

A cost center is a subunit or a department that handles costs. Its primary function is to manage operations to make sure they won't exceed budgetary projections. In other words, cost centers are corporate central nervous systems in charge of optimization and efficiency. They eliminate and sometimes create pain points in the administrative hurdle, establishing standard operating procedures (SOPs) for information control, procurement, distribution, order, and client support management.

In a cost center at a large corporation, the essential work is done behind curtains, where great operators are often the unsung heroes. Some of them are well paid if their technical expertise happens to sit at the core of the company's value creation system, such as in IT or compliance, security, database, or business intelligence infrastructure. However, even qualified professionals in those areas encounter fewer opportunities for upward mobility, and, on average, are paid less than people in sales or engineering roles, typical profit center job areas.

Profit Center Definition

A profit center is a generating center for revenues, profits, but also costs. Profit centers are the reason for which businesses are run. Without profit centers, it would be impossible for a business to perpetuate. As an example, we can use the sales department of a company. The sales department is a profit center because sales departments ensure how much revenue will be earned, how many expenses the organization should incur to sell the products or services, and how much profit the company should make as a result. Likewise, research and development (R&D) departments are also profit centers, as they guarantee the next pipeline of offers to increase the bottom line. In sum, product development and sales personnel are second to none at any enterprise strategically.

In a recent *Fortune* article, "The Black Ceiling: Why African-American Women Aren't Making It to the Top in Corporate America," Xerox's former CEO, Ursula Burns, a pioneer in being a minority leader at the helm of a Fortune 500 company, indirectly highlights the importance of joining the right internal ranks inside a corporation to succeed. When presenting reasons why women, in general, don't have the best shot at executive-level positions, Mrs. Burns claims they often find themselves limited to supporting roles that don't lead to CEO jobs in the corporate sector. In a direct quote, she says, "HR isn't going to get you there [the CEO role]. Communication and the arts aren't going to get you there. The juice lies with people who are close to the product and the money."[20]

Although the article approaches the challenges of minority workers, especially African American women, and their limited opportunities to experience strong career mobility, the underlying message is universal: The actions required for advancing professionally are virtually the same for everybody. Become a part of influential networks in core company areas that will advance your chance of promotion. Avoid the sidelines. It doesn't hurt to repeat: Stay close to the product or the money. If you are indeed career-focused and driven, you must figure out how to get onto the profit center side, where the big decisions are made and opportunities for recognition reside. Keep that in mind as part of your long-term strategy. You may start in a cost center until you develop the technical skills to move into middle management. From this point onward, however, you should acquire complementary people and political skills to keep moving. Use your CIA thinking and start targeting roles that will get you there.

FINDING "OSCAR-WINNING" PERFORMANCES

You get recognized in life by what you do and what you show. In most environments, you'll be surrounded by equally smart, dedicated people looking for the same career breaks as you. So, you need major achievements to stand out, or what I call Oscar-winning performances. When you deliver them, make sure your accomplishments somehow get into the grapevine when impressive and legitimate. Plus, never take credit for what you didn't do, and always give credit for superior work, as generosity and esprit de corps get you far.

Our brain operates with heuristics. We make mental shortcuts to arrive at conclusions based on limited, superficial information. Unique stories, therefore, help people create positive mental models about you, and when you accomplish something significant, others automatically associate your accomplishments with your qualities. In other words, the moment you gain notoriety for doing something difficult, you become a rising star. Do that consistently, and you become a hero. My goal with this advice, though, is more modest. It is to help you move up the ladder, learn valuable lessons, and strengthen your connections.

Professionally, some of the best career-accelerating moves come from managing difficult situations, solving complicated problems, or gaining precious points with demanding clients. Other classic avenues for impressive accomplishments come from skillful conflict management, mediation, or negotiation; it bears repeating that people forget details and actions, but they always remember your demeanor, behavior, and emotional posture in situations. Lose control once, engage in a heated argument, and everyone perceives you as explosive and uncooperative. The same goes for hurtful remarks or cynicism. At any hint of those and they'll peg you as bitter and negative, no matter how you justify your behavior.

However, an Oscar-winning performance must be substantial and capable of pushing the bottom line—saving costs or generating money for the organization by breaking into a new market, developing a new product or service, or negotiating a strategic partnership.

Every company builds myths and storylines to boost morale and create a sense of unity. These mythical stories of Oscar-winning performances impress new hires and remind rank-and-file employees of commonly held organizational values. Examples are visionary founders who went against all odds to challenge powerful competitors to win, or innovators whose pioneering dreams were mockery targets, given the whimsical nature of their ambitions. As such, your Oscar-winning performances can pay off for years as part of your brand-building process. They may include deploying new software, onboarding clients to a new platform, landing a lucrative contract with a player that takes the reputation of your company to a new level, or finding a groundbreaking process improvement that can save time or costs, or enhance the overall experience for workers and clients.

MANAGE YOUR PROFILE

Your reputation is everything. You always want to be the voice of reason, self-control, and positivity. Grueling hours, pressure, demanding clients, failure, and many other things can drive you to the brink of emotional distress. It's easy to lose hope and occasionally blow off some steam, but you just have to be extra careful as to when and where you do so.

A few essential tips: Always frame yourself in a positive light. People may forget what you do, but they will always remember how you behave—especially with them. Being polite, respectful, and professional are basic attributes to nurture a good professional network.

Moreover, we have three basic profiles: How we perceive ourselves, how others perceive us, and how our online images come across. Recruiters and talent managers dig for every single detail about you in the hiring process. LinkedIn has gained ground lately. For most companies and hiring managers, the second step immediately after a résumé screening is a checkup of the candidate's LinkedIn profile. Things to keep in mind: Learn how to craft an impressive LinkedIn profile, making smart use of the front page's "real estate" by promoting your relevant skills and experiences while focusing on accomplishments—not just tasks.

The profile picture is also important. Uploading a clean headshot with a neutral background is preferable. Some people advise that it's best not to use an image that's older than two years, but that's debatable. It's more important that the picture looks professional and showcases your personality. Use common sense. Check someone's profile in a position like the one you seek within the same industry. Remember the adage, "Dress for the job you want instead of the one you have."

Overinvest in Opportunities.

If previous, career-related experience is the golden ticket to the vault of professional growth, then jumping at a new opportunity is the equivalent of yanking your jail cell's key off a sleeping guard's belt. I can't stress enough the importance of being at the right place, with the right boss, and taking on the right assignments. One way to jump at a new opportunity is by building organizational awareness. You need to know what's happening not only in your department but across divisions. If the company is buying a new system, being within the first cohort of trained workers gives you a leg up in the onboarding and implementation process. Somehow you want to be the workflow expert in the new platform.

As mentioned, real earning power is limited to the positions closest to the product and the money, either directly involved in building the new product or selling to the end client. To put it simply, you want the projects that will get you closer to these ends on measurable tasks. In exchange, administrative duties usually have zero career-accelerating power, though you should keep them for essential or rapport-building purposes. Know that if you get stuck doing them at the expense of real growth, you've agreed to a bargain in which the odds are stacked against you.

CAREER STRATEGY WITH CIA THINKING

A strong professional profile is composed of a combination of people, task-based skills, knowledge, and experience. To achieve that, you must build your personal brand by mirroring a consumer brand, where your value proposition—unique training and experiences—and who you are—character and personality—are very distinguishable. Get the story right, and consciously pursue opportunities in fast-growth, high-potential industries that promote your narrative. Many talented people ignore storytelling and make career moves that don't add experiential value to their profiles or simply chose poor-fitting jobs for who they are. You can't be part of that crowd.

In addition to the narrative, your approach to career acceleration should include other mandatory items, such as keeping stock of who you are, having the ability to make long-term decisions, and operating with openness to feedback and criticism. That, plus the story, forms the bedrock of your unique career strategy.

Let's look at the "three Ps" that can make your profile stand out on a tactical level, the elements of your storytelling, plus behaviors top companies and hiring managers typically focus on.

Project Experience

Your project experience comprises the combination of your skills, experiences, and knowledge in specific areas. The more relevant your project portfolio is with regard to current market trends, the better. Your experience must be backed by results and by other people's assessments of what you bring to the table. This is where Oscar-winning performances in previous roles really pay off. As an order of business, make sure your contributions are meaningful and your results are documented.

Potential

Your career progression can say a lot about you. Hiring managers are always observant of the types of moves you made and how often you made them. Promotions within a single firm are viewed more favorably than job-hopping. In essence, your progression indicates how well you adapt, build trust, and deliver results.

Starting your career in a large company gives you, on average, a more robust learning experience. It's usually easier to start large and make your way into a midsize, fast-growing organization later than the other way around. The more politicized environments of large companies normally serve a great deal in sharpening C-suite grade communication and people skills. Under the same microscope, recruiters also look at stability, which is a measure of fit, consistency, and loyalty. Ideally, you want to have anywhere between three to five years of tenure per role or company, simply because it's hard to bring any impact on less than that. More than five, and it may communicate stagnation unless it involves a high-quality project. Furthermore, the caliber of companies and people you worked with also carry some weight. Aim for the best, shop companies for culture, credibility, and market positioning. Before choosing a job, if you're in a position to do so, ask yourself, "Is the company a leader, a strong contender?"

Presence

Presence encapsulates three elements in one: personality, demeanor, and image. Make good first impressions, carry a positive attitude, and speak with confidence. At this point, you know that a person of passion *always* stands out. So, demonstrate fire in the belly and sparkle in the eyes in your interactions.

Besides, your ability to influence and engage people at work is always monitored. Hiring managers are interested in how you solve problems, learn, and adapt. Since much of that comes from emotional intelligence and critical thinking, invest in CIA competencies to have that kind of credibility and presence.

YOUR TACTICAL APPROACH TO CAREER MANAGEMENT

Take control of your career, look at the big picture, and add meaningful projects to your brand while looking for high growth areas. Consider building expertise in marketing, branding, finance, strategy, and management.

Self-reflection tactic: Find two or three activities you're consistently good at or things that come naturally to you. Then add two or three more skills you've developed over time. Contrast them with your interests. Analyze how natural talents, developed skills, and passions align within your industry of choice.

A rewarding career experience demands the ideal environment, one where you're capable of deploying your best. To get results, spend time and energy finding workable solutions instead of ideal ones—those who seek perfection all the time lack the pragmatism necessary to do well in business. Moreover, spotting nuances, lending a good ear to contrarian thinking and crafting compromises almost always works better than rigid confrontation. If you plan to climb higher, keep that in mind.

PART

4

LEADERSHIP

Leadership is as much a popular topic as it is controversial. There are over fifteen thousand books in print with leadership as the central theme, plus thousands of released articles every year in social media, publishing, and academia.[21] But where does the fascination for leadership come from? What makes leadership so important, and why do leaders matter? Like all human affairs, leadership has a biological component.

Homo sapiens are social animals. We live to cooperate and communicate. Our brains are designed to store a staggering amount of information. What separates us from other animals is not the unusual ratio of brain size and body, but our capacity for imaginative, abstract thinking. While other species band together and collaborate in small, relatively close numbers, humans mobilize hundreds, thousands, and millions with the simple power of storytelling.

Our capacity to weave together constructs, myths, and narratives enables us to connect and work together—even with strangers—towards a common goal or vision. If nothing else, leaders are essential and always in high demand because they orchestrate this collaboration, often articulating compelling stories. Leaders understand the power of fiction. They're the myth architects (and sometimes the myth busters) that permeate our collective imagination. Corporations, money, laws, and economic, political, and social orders are examples of abstract creations that govern society's rules with no physical presence but prevalent manifestation in the material world.

Evolutionary biology aside, leadership activities have direct implications for our lives. As individuals, we're not only at the mercy of decisions made by leaders, but of the stories we choose to believe and the narratives that shape our collective consciousness. Although critical in orchestrating essential life matters as a human evolutionary instrument, the overall picture of leadership today is not a positive one. In fact, most organizations or groups are successful despite bad leadership, not because of their leaders. A few facts about leadership[22]:

- Studies reveal the base rate of managerial incompetence worldwide to be between 50 and 75 percent.
- The average percentage of CEOs let go within a three-year cycle at Fortune 500 companies is 50 percent or more.
- 75 percent of respondents to employee satisfaction surveys worldwide rank their immediate bosses as the most stressful elements of their jobs.
- An HBR study revealed that "healthy and respectful" working climates are present at only 30 percent of the businesses in the United States.
- 67 percent of IT projects fail to deliver on desired outcomes of functionality, time, and budget, making U.S. businesses spend roughly $55 billion annually on badly scoped, poorly executed projects.

If you believe that is a harsh assessment of leadership, try this quick test. Think about the people who led you in the past, leaders you had on any given group activity—sports, camp, school, businesses. Now count them. From the total, how many would you voluntarily choose to follow again? Most people determine that they would support 25 to 40 percent of the leaders they've encountered in their lives a second time. *Ouch!* If you're a leader conscious of the challenges in leading teams, you probably see this as unfair. If you're a follower, chances are you concur with the low approval rate in general. You're both right.

In reality, the stakes are always higher for people in positions of power. They are judged by different standards, and arguably should be. This is precisely what makes the act of leadership equally rewarding and challenging—and why those worthy of the role are the hardwired, tough-skinned, and ambitious kind of people who tend to give more, do more, and be more.

LEADERSHIP IS BOTH NATURE AND NURTURE

In publishing, academia, and media, the echoing question of leadership is always the same: Are great leaders born or made? The never-ending debate of nature versus nurture rests on the specific traits that form great leaders—as effective leadership is not only at the forefront of the most pressing human affairs in politics, economics, business, sports, arts, and entertainment, but evolving with society's transformations in these same areas. The more complex and connected the world becomes, the better human-centric leaders it needs, with more leadership flavors and styles flourishing in the process.

Among the people who practice, study, and research leadership, there are two dissonant voices. On one side are those who are vocal on the belief that individual traits, personality, character, and intelligence form the building blocks of a great leader. On the other are those who believe critical situations and real-life experiences create leaders by trial. As in many complex debates, the truth about leadership lies toward the middle. The confidence and experience that forges a great leader also capitalizes on individual traits—mostly character and personality. Lapses on either front create half-baked leaders. So, leadership, in the end, is both nature and nurture.

The Role of Leadership in Business.

Professional leadership is about serving and performing. It requires more energy, character strength, and intelligence than most activities. Correspondingly, competent leaders make top money in every industry.

In organizations, leaders are paid for two things: 1) to get results and 2) to build teams. Some leaders excel at the results part but prove themselves too disruptive and abrasive to build teams. Others are great at creating harmonious, respectful environments but are too timid to challenge people to superior results. In the end, born or bred, you must deliver on a combination of these two factors to be respected as a great leader.

As a framework, leadership exists in three realms: the leader, the followers, the environment. While moving independently, the synergy between these realms dictates whether results will be satisfactory, legendary, or even disastrous.

The most common reasons for failure in leaders are lack of self-awareness, lack of organizational awareness, lack of technical intelligence, lack of political intelligence, lack of teambuilding skills.

The most common reason for failure in followers is the presence of too many whining, disruptive, slacking, sycophant employees in a given group.

The most common reasons for failure in environment are competitive threats to the business or the organization. This might include mergers, acquisitions, turnaround initiatives, bankruptcies, natural disasters, government regulations, and so on. External factors can be overwhelming to the point that they beat talented, energetic leaders; failure is indeed a character-forming element of leadership and is inherent to the systemic feedback loop of leader-follower-environment. In the end, what makes a great leader is not the absence of failure but how one learns from it.

More than an authoritative position, a leadership mindset has never been more essential to propel a career. Modern companies are creating pivotal roles for independent leaders without the hierarchical duties of a functional manager. Global enterprises don't necessarily want managers of people but self-managed people who think and act like leaders. For instance, every time you serve your organization's mission in a way that generates tangible results that add value, you're acting as a leader. If you're making autonomous decisions that are sparking solutions, enhancements, or innovations, you're acting as one too. In essence, leadership is not about ruling or telling people what to do—it's about making inclusive, collaborative decisions.

Look critically at some contemporary mainstream corporate roles, and you realize most entry-level jobs at large companies today have many leadership components. Project

Manager, Program Manager, Systems Security Manager, Business Analyst, Financial Analyst, Account Manager. A quick LinkedIn search for popular associate roles quickly indicates that most four-year degree holders start as leaders in modern organizations based on job requirements. Companies expect to hire subject matter experts capable of contributing independently from the get-go, people who can coordinate resources, teams, and timelines with minimum supervision.

The nature of cross-functioning teams in global companies demands leadership at every level. For a long time, people could get away professionally by hiding behind red tape and bureaucracy. Not anymore. With organizations becoming nimble and customer-focused, leadership has changed from the bobblehead, bossy types of the past to the creative, thoughtful, autonomous taskmasters of today—a more adaptive leadership class for an interconnected age. Under this new handbook, you either become a leader on those terms or stick to dead-end staff functioning roles, always looking over your shoulder at every newly emerged technological turn.

Should You Become a Leader?

Thinking like a leader is the best strategy to carve a niche for yourself. From corporate career pros to autonomous entrepreneurs, most people gain admission to superior work experiences with a leadership mindset. Few things are as noble as embracing a larger purpose and helping others succeed.

Considering leadership rests both on personal skills and the environment, some thought-provoking questions to emerging professionals might include, "Can I really aspire to become a leader, even if I don't have leadership traits?" Or "Should I even care about developing skills that will lead me to the C-suite someday?" The answer depends on how far you want to grow professionally. With all its inherent benefits, leadership is not a walk in the park. It gets isolating at times, and it brings forward a tremendous amount of pressure and a number of existential riddles on the way to success.

We must recognize that being a leader of people is not for everyone. Leadership roles are limited, and competition for the best roles is fierce. Leadership is often a lonely endeavor. People will approach you with ulterior motives, and the higher you climb in the corporate structure, the harder it is to distinguish a trustworthy colleague from a self-serving one. Indeed, this shift in dynamic may cause even the most established working relationships to buckle. Sharp, wholesome colleagues surprisingly turn defensive, as the nature of working relationships changes when you become a leader. Your former peers transform as soon as they start reporting to you. When their organizational progress gets tied to your assessments, they tend to hold back their more honest thoughts from you, so much so that one of your major goals as a leader is to uncover unspoken truths.

In exchange, the advantage of leadership is the platform to make a larger, more significant impact than you could otherwise. When teamwork works, the personal satisfaction of being a leader is at its highest. There's a special feeling in turning things around, driving positive change, and allowing others to find purpose. Such achievements contribute to one's legacy.

Another perk of being a corporate leader is privileged access to information exclusive to the high-stakes table. In business, the closer you get to the decision-making groups, the more control of opportunities and projects you have, with more levers to make smart, well-informed career decisions for yourself and your team.

Also, in leadership roles, you have a face outside the organization, with open pathways to a broader professional network. Intelligence sharing and support are common among like-minded individuals equally struggling in high-pressure environments. The arm's length relationships you experience with subordinates smooth out among peers. Furthermore, most professionals' "next job" ventures often come from these exclusive leader networks.

Last is money. While many rewarding positions today are product-centric, most six-figure-plus jobs are allocated to supervisory, managerial, and executive level roles. Once you become a leader in change management, sales, or product development, more top dollar skills you acquire. The C-suite is rarefied. No more than 10 percent of talented professionals reach the executive level during their careers, on average. In other words, you become a hot commodity under the laws of supply and demand if you manage to get good quality leadership experiences.

MBA courses are popular because people want to fast-track their careers by learning leadership secrets. Everyone wants the gravy train—but, aside from the networking, the real benefit of an MBA program is not the prestige or the money-making opportunities, it's the self-discovery journey that leads to career purpose and the chance to define a leadership style that suits you. Money is above all else a consequence of fit, followed by meaningful work experiences. Leadership roles, by nature, are equipped with those experiences, and consequentially, outstanding career-accelerating power.

FOUR CLASSIC LEADERSHIP PROFILES

Before you build a high-performing team, you must learn how to support one. That means accounting for differences in leadership styles, especially your boss's. A successful leader-follower relationship demands you to know precisely how your boss operates, so you adapt to better serve the team.

By the same token, if you're already leading people, it's also your responsibility to adapt your communication delivery to followers. At the core of your success or failure lies a capacity to assess behaviors and see what image you're projecting. The four profiles here can help you detect the type of leader you've been. For instance, if the results you're getting are short of projections, there is a chance you're relying too much on a particular style that is disengaging your team. Here is the opportunity to find out.

The Technician

Technicians are the SMEs—or subject matter experts—of the world. They are highly analytical, precise, logic-driven, and have a superior sense of integrity and responsibility.

Skilled at optimizing resources and meeting deadlines, Technicians make great managers due to their controlled and disciplined natures. Their downfall, however, tends to be their self-righteous inflexibility, as their minds cling to logic and factual evidence so rigidly that it diminishes their ability to think outside of the box. So, while Technicians make great individual contributors and middle managers, they are not always the best fit for the ambiguous and unpredictable roles at executive level. Typically, Technicians are too rational to mobilize in strategic roles.

Things a Technician Craves

- Rules, procedures, guidelines, precision, efficiency, continuous improvement.

Typical Technician Roles

- Accountants, software, mechanical, electric, process engineers, researchers, business analysts, data scientists, corporate trainers.

Ways in Which Technicians Typically Fail

- Technicians tend to rely too much on hard data and logic to build consensus.
- Technicians resist operating outside procedures and clear-cut guidelines.
- Technicians tend to be self-righteous and dismissive of creatives.
- Technicians are frequently better individual contributors than collaborators. Their "don't do

feelings" approach lacks emotional intelligence for more politicized roles. However, technicians excel as mid-level managers and supervisors, mainly in analytical, precision, data-driven environments.

If You Are a Technician: How to Improve Your Style and Stay True to Yourself

- Learn how to embrace uncertainty and deviate from your comfort zone when needed. Not every solution is grounded on hard logic or science.
- Don't torture yourself (and others) over perfect solutions. Acceptable, pragmatic ones also lead to meaningful results in business. Your clients are more often interested in benefits, not exactly product features.
- Recognize people have different styles. Effective ingenuity in problem solving is as much creative and experimental in nature as it is analytical.
- Learn how to communicate with creatives when you cross-collaborate.

If You Are a Follower: How to Build Trust with a Technician

- Give them data and factual evidence before you try to argue a position or ask for support.
- Use rational, linear thinking in communication, bring undisputed numbers and facts to your stories and briefings.

The Diplomat

The Diplomat's primary goal is to preserve harmony and traditional structures. They work hard to avoid conflict. Despite their schmoozing and tactful communication abilities, Diplomat leaders struggle to make harsh decisions that may rock the boat. That includes reprimanding or firing low performers and taking more aggressive courses of action. Diplomats are amiable in communication, but their excessive political correctness often prevents them from being more assertive in moments of crisis. This is their downfall, as there are just too many of those moments in business.

Things a Diplomat Craves

- Respectful relationships, harmony, high-class behavioral attitude, sensitivity to others, observance of group norms.

Typical Diplomat Roles

- Client-facing roles, frontline supervisors, academic advisors, professors, career counselors, politicians.

Ways in Which Diplomats Typically Fail

- Diplomats avoid having tough conversations where they must provide blunt feedback and criticism.
- Diplomats are too cautious to call out, reprimand, or punish low performers.

- Diplomat friendliness and candor get in the way of authority and assertiveness.
- Diplomats are slow to make hard but strategically important decisions that will disrupt the existing group norms.

If You Are a Diplomat: How to Improve Your Style and Stay True to Yourself

- Look carefully at the costs of harmony. Your goal as a leader is to be trusted and respected, not exactly liked.
- Enforce norms and set expectations clearly.
- Protect your team's morale and set high standards. Be tough with free riders. Call them out when they don't meet expectations. If you must, replace them, or you may lose the entire team due to your lack of assertiveness.

If You Are a Follower: How to Build Trust with a Diplomat

- Operate with empathy, finesse, and sophistication. If you need to convince them of something, use a mix of rational analysis and passion.
- Talk about the contributions you can make to strengthen the team's position. Ask them how they feel about your ideas. Demonstrate that you're conscious of other people's feelings and how your actions affect the team.

The Driver

Drivers are taskmasters who operate with a specific agenda. They're high-energy, self-driven leaders who are ruthless in goal achievement. On the downside, drivers are controlling, type A personalities who can often be abusive when unrestrained. Drivers don't take "no" for an answer. Under pressure, it's not uncommon for a Driver to intimidate followers for adopting attitudes they see as critically harmful to the task at hand.

Things a Driver Craves

- Results, results, results. Drivers hate excuses and missed targets.

Typical Driver Roles

- Most corporate leaders from mid to senior level are Drivers. They're good at setting goals, and their targeted focus allows them to reverse engineer projects and follow through on tactical plans like no one else.

Ways in Which Drivers Typically Fail

- Drivers cause friction by their sole commitment to hitting targets.
- Drivers tend to have domineering personalities.
- The Driver's pragmatic, more aggressive style often clashes with Diplomats and Technicians who are slower to make decisions.

- Drivers, when unhinged, may cause resentment. Creative, autonomous collaborators often struggle to bring their best under a Driver's authoritarian leadership.

If You Are a Driver: How to Improve Your Style and Stay True to Yourself

- Step on the brakes sometimes. Realize your energy can push people to their limits and compromise your results.
- Elect a team member to be "the bad cop," so you don't get to be overly pushy. Save your assertiveness for when it's needed. Good quality results are sometimes better than astonishing one-offs. Balance goal orientation with team building.
- If you're an inveterate visionary desperate for greatness, consider becoming an entrepreneur. As one, you won't have to follow political guidelines that you haven't designed. Restrictive corporate environments sometimes can kill your best assets, energy, and ambition.

If You Are a Follower: How to Build Trust With a Driver

- Drink a Red Bull before coming to work. Jokes aside, demonstrate drive to your leader at every step of the way.
- Avoid philosophical discussions during your one-on-ones.

- Look for practical ways to contribute, stating your targets very clearly. Drivers are more interested in your actions than your feelings.

The Strategist

If the Technician is too self-righteous to build rapport, the Diplomat too soft to shake things up, and the Driver too disruptive, the Strategist strikes the perfect balance between inquiry and advocacy, making for an excellent leader. This leadership style blends the positives of the previous three styles: the Technician's logical approach, the social inclusivity of the Diplomat, and the Driver's unwavering grit and determination. Strategists use multiple inputs to chart a new course, but mostly, they project the tough empathy required to connect, inspire, and deliver on results. Because the Strategist is skillful at connecting individual and organizational needs, he/she is more tactful than the Driver in building emotional engagement.

A Strategist fully understands that organizational transformations cannot be separated from personal changes. Instead of bullying and threatening, moving fast, and breaking things, the Strategist overcomes resistance with compelling storytelling. She/he frames the work under a higher purpose, often with a big social goal attached.

Things a Strategist Craves

- Positive transformations that make society better.

Typical Strategist Roles

- At the higher rungs of most organizations where they set mission, vision, and policy. Strategists are the architects of storytelling.

Ways in Which Strategists Typically Fail

- They don't. At least not from a behavioral standpoint. Internally, the only way a Strategist fails is if the work pursued doesn't connect with a higher purpose. External factors can derail strategies, and often the best leaders fail for a myriad of reasons— but that's not what we're discussing here.

If You Are a Strategist: How to Improve Your Style and Stay True to Yourself

- For everyone, but mainly for the Strategist, finding fit is everything. Connect with a higher purpose, choose work that draws upon your talents and promotes your life's mission.

If You Are a Follower: How to Build Trust with a Strategist

- Show that you believe in the vision. Be a partner in fighting resistance. If you're backing up a Strategist, chances are you're already working with change management transformations that will face tons of pushback and naysaying. Tough skin, then, is part of your job description.

Red Flags

Watch for these signs that might indicate your leadership style is failing by drifting too close to Technician, Diplomat, or Driver styles.

- You believe you're right and others are wrong most of the time.
- Your descriptions of reality don't quite sync with others' perceptions of the same events.
- You dread changes and are mostly playing catch-up to them.
- When things go south, you're quick to point out what others could have done differently.
- You frequently think people are failing your expectations.
- Your recent interactions with others have been frustrating, argumentative, and accusatory.
- You spend more time putting out fires than implementing new ideas.
- You struggle to connect your daily activities with a higher purpose.
- You avoid having tough conversations or issuing warnings, expecting your low performers to improve on their own at some point.

FOUR CLASSIC FOLLOWERSHIP PROFILES

Every person in a position of authority was once a follower or plays a followership role in some other area. Supervisors report to managers, managers report to directors, directors report to VPs, and CEOs report to the board of directors. Even entrepreneurs, bastions of the independent spirit, report to investors. So, whether to fine-tune your progression from follower to leader or simply to become a more effective one, getting a grasp on followership types will enable you to advance further. On average, a manager must deal with four types of followers based on performance and relationship levels.

The Public Relations

Public Relations followers display good instincts and political awareness. They are superior readers of emotional currents, and skillful in assessing the team's overall feelings towards initiatives. Public Relations are quick to detect who's on board and who's not. Invariably, they are strategic assets for a leader to have, considering their loyalty and people skills.

Although having a loyal sounding board with eyes and ears on the ground is beneficial, a leader who surrounds himself with too many Public Relations followers may experience declining results over time. That's because, by nature and temperament, this type of follower spends too much time in relationships and not enough in execution. Public Relations also tend to say "yes" to everything the boss says, creating poor leadership accountability. Since bad decisions are neither questioned nor reviewed, they keep coming.

The Automaton

The Automaton is the typical "just tell me what to do" type of follower—the kind of person who's not that skillful and is a mere bureaucrat with no engagement or particular loyalty to the leader and the overall direction of the team. For the Automaton, a job is nothing more than a paycheck. He/she works fiercely not to rock the boat and keep things as simple as they are. Automatons are lifers in organizations, and they tend to do well in highly hierarchical, predictable machines that are slow to change.

The Hired Gun

The Hired Gun follower works hard to master a craft and reach goals. They're great Technicians who develop subject matter expertise over time but don't necessarily want to rub shoulders or build personal relationships with anybody, including their bosses. Hired Gun followers have no patience or sensitivity to interpersonal dynamics. These lone wolves perform at a high level and seldomly take the initiative, often waiting on the sidelines for clear-cut directions. While their track record on results is excellent, their long-term legacy on relationships is flawed.

The Copilot

The Copilot follower combines the Public Relations commitment to loyalty and good relationships with the Hired Gun's extra drive for results. Like Public Relations, Copilot followers buy into the leader's overall vision. However, their advantage is the natural impetus to solve problems and execute plans, embodying the ideal follower for a thriving leader to have on his or her side. Copilots believe in bringing impact. They hold their leaders accountable for decisions, questioning them and providing input when opportune.

A few takeaways from this model:

- The leader is responsible for creating the environment.
- The environment dictates the followership types a leader will foster.
- All four types have their purpose in specific situations.
- Organizational culture, resources, and a leader's capacity to mobilize and engage also play a part in the quality of followers in each context.
- A leader may foster a balanced distribution of types among his base, but real change doesn't happen without Copilots.

THE COUSINS

In the same way a manager has the responsibility to foster the right mix of followers, he or she is also in charge of developing them across these typical profiles, gradually shifting followers from more disruptive to more productive types—or replacing them when that is not possible.

Since we first looked at these profiles under the dimensions of performance and relationship, we can now frame them under critical thinking and engagement dimensions. For instance, followers who score high on critical thinking challenge things and feel responsible for finding new solutions. On the flip side, followers who score low on critical thinking expect their managers to find all the answers. As for engagement, highly engaged followers work hard and are proud of their contributions to the team's success. In exchange, poorly engaged followers don't have the same stamina, pride, and willpower, working cleverly and diligently to shield themselves from more work and responsibility. So, when unhinged and poorly managed, the four original followership profiles may turn into the following:

Yes-Men

These are highly engaged followers who display limited critical thinking. As the direct cousin of Public Relations, Yes-Men work from a standpoint of seeking to preserve harmony. They are consistently trying to please their bosses rather than challenging things. The net result is a complete absence of originality. As risk-averse, often insecure individuals, Yes-Men are highly dependent on their bosses for direction.

To turn Yes-Men into Copilots, bosses must tap into their technical skills, considering these types are dutiful and knowledgeable but lack the confidence to operate independently. While quick to detect problems, Yes-Men are less inclined to offer solutions. Thus, it's the leader's role to engage them in problem-solving. Only when Yes-Men wear an analytical lens and ultimately find the courage to propose solutions will they effectively contribute without overtaxing their leader.

The Lazybones

Automaton's first-degree cousins, Lazybones are followers who display low levels of engagement and critical thinking. Teams formed by Lazybones are a recipe for disaster as they fail on both dimensions. Lazybones show their true colors when they make tons of excuses for not getting work done. A typical workplace situation is when a Lazybones disappears for hours in useless chatting and socializing in some dark corner of the building, articulating clever ways to avoid finishing assignments while appearing busy.

Contrary to what many believe, Lazybones have tons of motivation—just on things outside of work, such as hobbies, families, and relationships. Ultimately, they work for the money in order to attend to these other things.

Ideally, managers should focus on getting rid of Lazybones instead of engaging them. Turning one into a Copilot is tough, as in Hawaii's Ironman World Championship tough. Often, though, Lazybones are not a completely lost cause. Sometimes finding a different role more aligned with their interests can spark some motivation and save a career. As an integrity model, a good leader must do that, even for benefits to be reaped elsewhere. Ultimately, a leader needs results. One of a leader's primary duties is to improve performance. That includes finding ways to engage and develop people or fighting hard to replace them when this is not possible.

The Crybaby

This is a knowledgeable, articulate, and experienced follower who at some point was a Copilot, but for whatever reason—bypassed for promotion, didn't get a raise, got reassigned to a different team—went sour and turned into a bitter creature.

Like Hired Guns, Crybabies score high on critical thinking, but they're out of synch emotionally. They're the first to point out—and talk about—their leader's faults and their organization's shortcomings. They're experts on what the company is "doing wrong" and all the reasons why the ship will sink. As professional naysayers, this type of follower is often a missionary in search of new converts. As misery loves company, Crybabies are dangerous to any team. Over time, their poisonous attitude anchors morale. Managers should keep an eye on them.

Mainly, a Crybaby follower craves recognition. A leader who sees value in a Crybaby's contributions and has tools to assign more rewarding tasks should approach this type of follower with a game-changing plan. After all, honest face-to-face conversations might lead to movie-like transformations that sometimes happen in real life too. But if the bitterness is too ingrained, or the naysaying beyond salvation, then a replacement is the only alternative before the Crybabies' ranks replicate Gremlin style and the leader gets the boot instead.

The Self-Starter

A fully engaged follower who is passionate about the team and its goals. Direct cousin of the Copilot, the Self-Starter works hard to bypass challenges and achieve results, often operating autonomously to promote the team. Due to their high levels of critical thinking and engagement, Self-Starters tend to make sound independent decisions that respect their leader's values and vision.

To keep Self-Starters engaged, leaders must provide them enough freedom and latitude to operate. As over-achievers and high-performers, Self-Starters expect regular coaching and feedback. It's essential for them to feel they are making progress and experience the impact of their contributions. Also, Self-Starters are energized by challenges, including promotions and additional responsibilities.

Though Self-Starters can be amazing ingredients to high-performing teams, they're also demanding and impatient. If they somehow feel progress is too slow or bosses don't bring them excitingly enough projects, they may leave. Self-Starters have options, especially inside organizations where their individual qualities are well known.

A few takeaways from this model:

- The four stages of followership are not rigid—people transition among them during their careers.
- Some bosses are tempted to delay the conversion of Yes-Men to Self-Starters because of fragile egos and the extra work required for engagement.

- The more time people spend in the same role or organization, the more likely they are to become Crybabies.
- Company selection processes should detect people's likelihood of becoming Automatons and Lazybones before hiring.
- While leaders should deal promptly with Automatons and Lazybones, organizations should evaluate their leadership classes constantly. Sudden spikes in both ranks often indicate bad leadership.

These leadership and followership profiles highlight some of the challenges involved in creating high-performing teams, where a well-oiled machine stems from three factors:

1. The individual qualities of the leader
2. The personality, knowledge, and interests of the followers
3. The nature of the environment

When the minimum requirements are met for the environment—tools and resources to engage and motivate, quality projects for followers, a considerable number of talented, ambitious, well-mannered people—a competent leader can spearhead greatness. When these raw ingredients are absent, even competent leaders are subject to failure. Conversely, incompetent leaders who lack vision or people skills can also squander quality resources and destroy engagement, creating a team full of bickering Automatons and Lazybones in the process.

HOW THE FOLLOWERSHIP PROFILES ADVANCE IN THEIR CAREERS

Public Relations and Yes-Men tend to do well, considering the value relationships have in career advancement. In the end, though, their destiny is harnessed to the people in power whose favors they've won. When the tide turns and that person is no longer in charge to protect them, Public Relations and Yes-Men don't have sufficient results to leverage. Sometimes it's just too much politics and not enough action with them.

Hired Guns and Crybabies rise to a point but often get stuck in the middle. As talented contributors, they establish successful careers as contractors, consultants, or independent providers. However, this group's lack of political skills often narrows their career scope.

Automatons and Lazybones spend their entire careers frustrated without making any meaningful progress. These followers are the most vulnerable to technological changes. Although needed for clerical work, Automatons and Lazybones don't bring any personal touch to their work. For that reason, companies are constantly trying to automate them. Sooner or later, they find a way.

Copilots and Self-Starters ultimately rise to the top of their chosen careers, invariably becoming great leaders themselves. Their balanced results and relationship orientation leave a shiny string of Oscar-winning performances behind, solidifying their brands and exposing them to special learning and growing opportunities. The Copilot's and Self-Starter's competence and political skills also align them well for entrepreneurial activities.

WHAT ATTRIBUTES ARE COMPANIES SEEKING IN THOUGHT AND PEOPLE LEADERS?

A professional may have outstanding credentials, such as prestigious degrees and world-class experiences. Yet, as the technological, regulatory, and competitive landscapes of businesses continues to evolve, executives must adopt both learning and adaptability strategies to survive.

All things being equal, adaptability may be a better predictor of success than experience and education now. In general, executive search companies carefully mine success stories in adaptability and quick studies for recruiting. How you bring results during challenging circumstances is of particular interest.

Historically, talent selection went through three different anthropological waves. During the first, people looked for physical attributes as a leading indicator of performance. Strength, fitness, and health mattered most for what constituted societies' primary needs in the first millennium—construction, military, and agriculture. To some degree, our subconscious is still biased in that regard. Recent studies pointing to people in leadership roles as being taller on average are probably one lingering indicator of those primitive times.[23]

The second post-industrial revolution wave took hold during most of the twentieth century. As work became standardized, it demanded that workers be more verbal and analytical, with standardized intelligence coefficients forming the backbone indicator of who would thrive or fail in a corporate setting.

More recently, technology made work more complex. Companies started emphasizing the need for specific behavioral competencies. Recruiters in the process adopted a compartmentalized criterion with a shortlist of attributes and characteristics, breaking jobs into smaller clusters of critical competencies. This is the process today, where the norm is to recruit for personality, education, and experience.

Now, with the rise of artificial systems, we're entering a fourth wave where versatility and learning potential are central. The U.S. Bureau of Labor Statistics now estimates that average professionals will change jobs from ten to fifteen times during their careers. In short, what will drive job access in the robot-accelerated age are attributes such as flexibility, adaptability, and infinite learning.

In addition to change management success stories, companies look for the following traits when staffing for leadership:

- Strategic orientation
- Customer orientation
- Influencing skills
- Talent development skills
- Team leadership skills
- Change management skills
- Market insights

On a tactical plan, what strategies can you adopt for a shot at leadership roles? First, understand the power of results. Focus on achievements. Performing billable work is the fastest way to earn stripes. Technical, sales, and leadership are skills learned on the job, where the school of hard knocks is the best learning institution. Stretch assignments and mentorship are the best tools for in-house development, especially in large companies. Harness storytelling. Create narratives about your trials. What lessons have you learned? What victories you had? What can you accomplish going forward? Use the insights you gain for building résumés, cover letters, and interview material.

NEW DEMANDS ON MANAGERS OF PEOPLE

Managing your work is simple. Managing others is not. To complicate things, talent management responsibilities are now gradually shifting to functional managers despite the fact that this has historically been an HR domain. Flattening organizations' dynamics of cost and performance explain the trend. One irrefutable argument is that managers can better handle recruiting, retention, and performance reviews since they're closer to the action than HR partners.

Returns on human capital are more difficult to predict than returns on equipment. When it comes to talent needs, the first impulse is to hire. In large U.S. companies, 60 percent of roles are sourced externally. That figure used to be 10 percent a decade ago.[24] In that regard, companies can follow one of three strategies: buy talent, build talent, or borrow talent via contracting.

Hiring is expensive when you factor in costs, not just in compensation but in output. Companies are forced to pay market rates, and outsiders take on average three years to perform at their internal counterparts' levels. In exchange it takes, on average, seven years for internal hires to close the pay gap against external candidates,[25] which means internal people are constantly shortchanged.

Borrowing talent is not cheap either, when you add the searching and agency costs that go with hiring a contractor. What usually makes contracting work even more costly is that companies often hire contractors for essential functions rather than ad hoc projects, making it challenging to eliminate them in a downturn.

In sum, although it is riskier, building talent is less costly than hiring it. Your talent needs today may be different tomorrow. Plus, your capacity to retain exceptional people puts more pressure on creating environments that incentivize them to stay. You're simply forced to raise the bar.

Your Battle of Marathon as a leader is to build and sustain high-performing teams. On that note, how do you become a magnet for talent? Corny as it is, select the best you can find and help them succeed. Simple, but difficult. That includes spotting individuality and assigning the right projects to the right people. Other actions to take on your leadership quest include the following:

- Build and sustain trust.
- Form a team of complementary skills, bringing in talents that help address your weaknesses.
- Lead by example, share your goals, explain what you're working towards.

- Understand that everything you do or don't do in a leadership role impacts morale.
- Strike the balance between pushing too hard or too little. Push too hard, and you may lose support, but push too little, and you may lose on results.
- Support people at the top and help them succeed—managing up is one of your priorities. Executive leaders oversee the high-caliber project pipeline. Keep them happy.
- Don't solely rely on hard data and metrics. Talk to your team to uncover issues.
- Be humble, learn how to operate with "gray," and take calculated risks.

If we look at leadership as a mix of nature and nurture, with one-third being natural abilities—intelligence, personality, temperament—and two-thirds being training and experience, we can also point to other qualities great leaders possess in general:

- Good mix of intelligence and people skills
- Self-awareness, organizational awareness
- Solid technical knowledge and experience
- Energy, grit, and tough skin
- Confidence, optimism, positive attitude
- Superior communication, presentation skills
- Sound judgment and integrity

Superior leaders, for the most part, are high-octane overachievers. But not all high-octane overachievers are leaders. In general, the most productive people in business display consistency, drive, technical knowledge, and problem-solving and collaborative abilities. Except for collaboration, none of these guarantee leadership success. When you lead, what matters most is an openness to change, the capacity to develop others, and clear communication. In other words, insane adaptability, communication, and political skills.

WHY SHOULD PEOPLE FOLLOW YOU? EIGHT COMMON TRAITS FOR SUPERIOR LEADERSHIP

Starting with the two premises established so far, 1) leadership is part nature, part nurture, and 2) leadership styles are eclectic and situation-based, it's safe to say that there isn't a ready-made recipe for securing and inspiring followers. However, you can improve your chances if you demonstrate certain traits.

You're human and imperfect. Everyone has weaknesses and insecurities. People relate more to those who show vulnerabilities than to those who pretend to be perfect. Be candid about some of your shortcomings. Don't be afraid to admit you don't have all the answers. Invite your followers to propose solutions. Engage them to bring fresh perspectives to problems.

You hone your sensors. Throughout your career, critical information won't always be shared or openly expressed. Stay tuned for mixed signals and develop a sixth sense.

Your ability to make sound decisions with incomplete data gives you credibility. While anyone can read charts, only exceptional leaders use intuition as a tool. Even fewer are bold enough to make decisions on a hunch.

You're authentic. Most people take years to discover what makes them unique. Nothing is more boring than a bland conformist. Whether through a handshake, a visual cue, or a dress style, superior leaders always find ways to stand out. They create brands to communicate personal experiences, beliefs, and values that reveal what they stand for in life. Communicate with authenticity. While you may learn from other leaders' experiences and occasionally adopt some of their tricks, leadership has many voices. To win, you must find yours.

You're self-aware. We've discussed the value of knowing yourself extensively throughout this manual. If anything, it serves to find the most critical career-acceleration element—fit. A self-aware person rarely takes a job for money. One looks for purpose, talent compatibility, and career goal alignment. Likewise, self-awareness helps you stay grounded. It strikes the balance between being overly critical with yourself and a delusional optimist. Define who you are and who you want to become. Once you discover who that is, don't ever settle for anything less than being that person in everything you do.

You're self-controlled. When you control your triggers and keep negative emotions at bay, you act with reason. Only when you do so will you create an environment of trust and respect—the superglue for a highly productive team to exist. Manage your impulses. Watch your language. Trust the power of words. Even when speaking to yourself, don't allow negativity to creep in.

You have inner drive. Inner drive to work for long-term goals beyond money and status are common traits of both world-class professionals and influential leaders. Motivation is a factor that really resonates when you find purpose. Until you do, work is mostly burdensome. Find your motivation and set the bar high. Then keep rowing towards meaningful results. Your career will thank you.

You show tough empathy. Leaders should give people what they need, not just what they want. Numerous leadership scenarios demand you to push boundaries and stretch people for their benefit. Too many potential leaders waste energy trying to be liked. Instead, real leaders focus on being trusted. The added benefit of tough empathy is the indication to others that you operate by high standards, that you care about the tasks and the organization. Be strict but respectful. Give people a voice. You don't have to follow suggestions all the time, but always listen.

You're skilled in conflict management. In both business and life, conflict is inevitable. The world does not operate by your values. Like people and political skills, conflict management is a leadership skill that helps you compromise. You won't always have things to your exact specifications, so be ready to negotiate on common needs, not positions. Hone your persuasive powers. While you may have all the motivation and empathy in the world, you cannot get results without dexterity in conflict management.

WELL-ROUNDED LEADERSHIP COMPETENCIES

Leadership talks are like drinking water out of a firehose—*overwhelming*. There are an abundance of things you're being told to do and so many qualities you're being told to embody. The last thing you should be adding to your list of stressors is that of impostor syndrome. A bit of insecurity is customary and even expected at this point. No one is ever ready to be a leader until they step into the challenge. To humanize things, maybe it's worth looking at leadership competencies under these four practical lenses while using your inner voice.

My performance leadership, where I'm the visionary. Here I push for excellence in results. I spend a considerable amount of time studying, practicing, and developing expertise in business areas where I can add value—financial, technological, or political—and where I excel and perform higher than the average person.

My interpersonal leadership, where I learn how to build relationships. Here I hone my political skills to navigate the organization. I manage expectations at all levels, I build solid teams, I communicate with energy, I deliver killer ten-minute presentations.

My intrapersonal leadership, where I care about developing myself and striving for more. Here, I invest in self-development, I build character, I find the strength to persevere, and I adapt to any situation by being flexible and being willing to improvise.

My change leadership, where I adopt an entrepreneurial spirit. Here, I am the driver of transformative changes, not the person who's just putting out fires. My insights find, assimilate, and lead the strategic course the group takes. I don't just talk about getting things done—I take action and make sure it happens.

Final Leadership Checklist

As you operate as a leader in any capacity or role, ask yourself these questions periodically: "When I think like a leader, I . . ."

- Embrace the new—ideas, projects, changes.
- Maintain an absurdly high level of integrity—I don't know anybody who wants to work with a person they don't respect or trust.
- Take full responsibility for my department's success—the person who says "This is not my job" is scratched for good.
- Practice emotional intelligence and self-control.
- Study time management to be more productive than the average person—to the point I join the selected 10 percent best in a class (a.k.a. world-class) professional group.
- Play by the rules but accept that I'm competing for a promotion, so I stay competitive.

- I worry about getting better more than I worry about being good.
- I work toward long-term goals; whatever I'm facing today won't stop me from achieving them.
- I speak with brevity and intent; my body language communicates respect but firmness. When I talk, I'm thoughtful and convincing.

5

TECHNICAL DOMAIN LEVEL SKILLS

Research and history show a meaningful, rewarding job gives you a sense of purpose and self-worth. The overall benefits derived from a carefully orchestrated career haven't changed, but the approach and preparation required to find one have. Digital age careers require a new set of skills and strategic focus, as competition for good, well-paying jobs is not only fierce but *globally* fierce. The last thing you want is to compete in a race to the bottom, always against the latest revolution in automation or lower-cost outsourcing option. As the CEO of Gallup, Jim Clifton illustrates in his book *The Coming Jobs War*, "The primary will of the world is no longer about peace, freedom, or even democracy. The will of the world is first and foremost to have a good job."[26]

If we were to crunch this entire book into a series of short-form, actionable strategies, it would be: Take control of your career, look at the macro trends shaping the future of work, build relationships around a professional community, and fight fiercely for projects that enhance your brand. To effectively use those strategies and make an impact that speaks to you at your core, you also need an intellectual toolbox equivalent to what the best digital age professionals have—one that includes, to a minimum, the following four groups of skills and competencies.

GROUP ONE: BASIC TOOLING SKILLS

Even for entry-level corporate and service roles, a minimum of "tech savviness" is expected—at least enough to navigate Microsoft Office Suite, Apple's iOS, and remote work collaborative tools such as Zoom, BlueJeans, and Slack. Lately,

Google G Suite applications—Drive, Meet, Hangouts, and Gmail—are becoming not just ubiquitous, but mandatory, so much so that *Inc.* magazine recently revealed that 31 percent of Microsoft Office 365 users also utilize Google products at work.

To a digital native, this may seem redundant, but many non-digital pros struggle with basic applications, including remote connections, tokens, email rules, desktop formatting, and options. While I assume this is too basic for most people, we can't stress enough the importance of having basic tech savviness in a modern workplace.

Other notable tech tools and makers in vogue include Amazon Web Services (AWS), Atlassian's suite of products—Confluence, Jira, and Trello—and Salesforce. This latter is not only used for customer relationship or account management, but also for remote collaboration solutions with their acquisition of Slack Technologies. If you've worked in cross-collaborative enterprise software projects, chances are you're at the very least familiar with these tools.

On top of that, mastery of social media etiquette for content creation and posting is becoming mainstream. For instance, people are gradually unlocking the value of LinkedIn to network and showcase their expertise, often sharing interesting tidbits about their company and specific contributions made at work. Posting, sharing, and commenting on topics relevant to your industry can help promote your brand.

Examples of essential technology tools to master:

- Microsoft Office Suite
- Apple's iOS
- Google G Suite

- Remote collaboration tools
- Digital dashboards, customer support tools, project management tools, order management systems, enterprise resource planning systems

GROUP TWO: UNIVERSAL SKILLS

Polished leadership skills, communication, and innovative thinking are a minimum requirement in navigating a career track towards world-class performance. Other subcategories of important skills to refine include negotiation, information analysis, organization, problem solving, time management, and empathy. If anything, everyone must know how to behave in a professional setting, which thus also includes understanding essential norms and principles universally applicable to the workplace.

While most people use the terms skills and competencies interchangeably, competencies sit at a higher level than skills. An example: Effective public speaking is considered a communication skill. A competence, conversely, is adapting your communication style for each occasion. You're good at public speaking with large or small crowds, you're masterful on one-on-one conversations, you excel at small talk, and you write excellent content, both in short and long form. Combined, those skills make you a uniquely competent communicator.

Examples of universal skills and competencies to master:

- Leadership
- Communication

- Time management
- Discipline
- Negotiation
- Creativity
- Problem solving

Ultimately, you should craft your own list of competencies beyond that. If you're lacking ideas, remember you can always pull a Picasso—look for great people in action, emulate their behaviors, ask questions, and find a mentor.

GROUP THREE: BUSINESS SKILLS

Don't be fooled by smoke screens, fancy terms, or acronyms. Regardless of the technological degree, scale, or scope, a business enterprise's functioning is very straightforward. Whichever contributions you'll make in business, they will invariably fall into creating or building the offer, selling it, or managing operations around its proposal, including aspects of communication and public relations.

Businesses exist to centralize resources in design, production, communication, distribution, and fulfillment. Big ideas help companies market a vision of innovation and extraordinariness while they make money on the mundane. To illustrate, for all the buzz on self-driving cars, virtual reality glasses, and other supposedly stellar applications, Alphabet (Google), to this day, really makes money selling keywords to advertisers. Estimates point to 80 percent of their revenues coming from that vertical alone.[27] The same goes for Facebook; with all its diversification and acquisitions—Instagram, WhatsApp, and others—the company's primary revenue source comes from digital ads.

Globally, businesses are harnessing the power of digital tools to collect, organize, and use data for decision-making. In consequence, companies are centralizing their business models around data processing and platform applications. As data becomes the digital economy's currency, corporate money is channeled to product areas. Master skills in technical project or product management, and you'll experience booming career acceleration. Most career growth in the 2020s will come from product verticals, with software and supporting applications offering solid pockets to specialize in.

The growth trajectory of technology for business is relatively new. Organizations will be rolling out new waves of platforms and data operations within the decade. Think of all the legacy systems companies will push to upgrade and the new lines of businesses that will proliferate from acquired, merged, or proprietary software tools. As a result, digital applications will seamlessly dictate business strategy. While enterprises in general may be on different integration stages, every company will invest in incremental growth.

Marketing, finance, and business development are also positioned for growth alongside technology as core areas of expertise. Like HR, customer support, and admin, those classic enterprise verticals are perennial. Despite clever new job titles and descriptions, such functional roles remain intact in organizations, as today's businesses operate in much the same way, albeit on a different scale and speed, as businesses from the past.

Examples of business skills to master:

- Budgeting and finance
- Business development and sales
- Marketing and communications
- Product development
- Programming
- Designing

GROUP FOUR: INDUSTRY-RELATED SKILLS

From oil and gas to healthcare and retail, from media and entertainment to professional services, industry skills change significantly between jobs. That is the main reason career transitions become particularly challenging over time. In a sense, you may become a victim of your success as your entrenched knowledge pushes you deeper and deeper into a specific line of work.

As a rule, stick to career tracks where you benefit from cumulative expertise and training, not only in tooling and applications but also in image, approach, and culture, and in areas where you clearly understand the landscape and the rules of engagement. Meanwhile, keep developing universal and business-specific skills to save you from pigeonholing.

In general, once you settle on a swim lane, industry skills are the easiest to parlay into growth but the hardest to unpeg from when you need to change. For example, it's easier, in general, to switch industries in IT, finance, marketing, legal, and human resources functions, and much harder in R&D, engineering, product, and sales areas. For similar reasons, switching from "business to business" to "business to consumer" (B2B to B2C) and vice-versa is quite challenging due to the difference in business models, product knowledge, and relationships you establish along the way.

Here are some examples of specialized industry skills to master:

- Mobile and cloud platform architecture, governance and documentation (tech)
- Data privacy, compliance, and cybersecurity (business)
- Video and editing (marketing)
- Sales and content (marketing)
- Telecommunications (business)
- Engineering design software (tech)
- Data science (tech)
- Natural language processing (tech)
- Automation (tech)
- Robotics (engineering/tech)
- Data management (mix of tech and business)
    - Search engine optimization
    - Marketing analytics
    - Business analytics

THE 70 PERCENT RULE

Leading consultants, headhunters, and executive placement professionals correlate earning potential directly with practical experiences in a field. Empirical evidence points to professional learning coming, on average, 70 percent from direct work experience, 20 percent from applied coaching and mentoring, and 10 percent from formal education and training.

Looking at the exorbitant costs of education and the worldwide proliferation of online certification platforms, we realize most people look for education to boost earnings, tapping into the less significant fraction of the knowledge base. Instead, your approach should be different. Yes, invest in education—but also find project-based experiences to accelerate your career at the beginning. After all, they pay you for what you know, and 90 percent of that does not come from school or formal training.

Managing your career requires you to define roles and industries of interest—particularly roles at hipo areas. Today, most careers are grounded in the construction of digitized products or entrenched business verticals with dominating elements of design, media creation, marketing, branding, strategy, and management, mostly of intangible resources, but to no small degree of people.

At this point, we can consolidate the notion of fit as crucial—meaning you absolutely need the right setting, the right culture, and the right environment to thrive. Your career success mostly depends on making intelligent choices about jobs. Here are a few things to ask yourself when evaluating opportunities.

- Can you accomplish the primary mission for which they're hiring based on your experience and skills?

- Who's your new boss? Can you relate to that person? Do you believe you'll be able to develop a nurturing relationship of trust and respect with her/him?
- Who else is on the team? What's your assessment of the overall talent?
- Do you know what kind of financial resources you'll be given in order to succeed? It's tough to bring a measurable impact on underfunded company areas.
- How does your style align with the organizational culture? Are you a whimsical creative getting into a rigid, top-down command space? Conversely, are you a rule-abider stepping into a freewheeling, chaotic one?
- How does the job promote your long-term goals? Will you learn something of market value? Will you develop any expertise you'll need at some point?
- Will you be proud to say that you work for this company?

While we touched on the merits of lifelong, universal principles to succeed, we also highlighted the importance of domain expertise. The concept of the T-shaped individual prescribes scope, eclecticism, and multifacetedness as essential. Yet, you must pair these with in-depth technical credentials for a world that's gradually becoming more fractured and hyperspecialized.

Most corporate jobs still require a college education. But as we'll see in this section, credentials are gradually outpacing degrees as a requirement for employment in high-growth areas. For that reason, we'll look at trade-based training options to be paired with a four-year degree—or even to implement before a degree, if you're still exploring options. Whichever the case, your preparation must deliver on the most precious asset for kickstarting or pivoting in your career—*a tangible project portfolio to showcase your talents and get you hired.*

THE FUTURE OF JOBS

The World Economic Forum (WEF), one of the world's most influential international non-governmental organizations (NGOs) for public and private partnership, releases highly anticipated economic reports. Recently, they published two analyses that received extensive publicity. The first, *The Future of Jobs Report 2018,* points to mobile, cloud, big data, and artificial intelligence as the four leading drivers of disruption to the contemporary world of work. The report projects intense job growth in emerging professions related to these combined segments to increase from 16 to 27 percent of total global employment by 2020. High-paid roles on the rise as part of this trend include data analysts and scientists, software and application developers, and e-commerce and social media specialists across industries.

The second WEF report, *Jobs of Tomorrow, Mapping Opportunity in the New Economy 2020,* covers the impressive rise of health care, people and organization, creative media production, and green economy jobs. The analysis organizes emerging careers into seven professional clusters to which economists believe major economic output and 6.1 million new global positions will open by 2023. It then pairs each cluster with corresponding LinkedIn job posts and skills listed for these group areas in the platform, where they mapped the twenty roles with the highest growth across twenty major economies worldwide. The byproduct is seven distinct occupational clusters with specific role and skill requirements, as follows.

Top Roles and Top Ten LinkedIn Skills across All Roles for Each Professional Cluster

1 - Data and Artificial Intelligence	
Jobs	*Skills*
1. Artificial intelligence specialist 2. Data scientist 3. Data engineer 4. Big data developer 5. Data analyst 6. Analytics specialist 7. Data consultant 8. Insights analyst 9. Business intelligence developer 10. Analytics consultant	1. Data science 2. Data storage technologies 3. Development tools 4. Artificial intelligence 5. Software Development Life Cycle (SDLC) 6. Management consulting 7. Web development 8. Digital literacy 9. Scientific computing 10. Computer networking

2 - Engineering and Cloud Computing	
Jobs	*Skills*
1. Site reliability engineer	1. Development tools
2. Python developer	2. Web development
3. Full stack engineer	3. Data storage technologies
4. Java script developer	4. Software Development
5. Back end developer	Life Cycle (SDLC)
6. Frontend engineer	5. Computer networking
7. .Net software developer	6. Human computer
8. Platform engineer	interaction
9. Development specialist	7. Technical support
10. Cloud engineer	8. Digital literacy
11. DevOps engineer	9. Business management
12. Cloud consultant	10. Employee learning &
	development

3 – People and Culture	
Jobs	*Skills*
1. Information technology recruiter	1. Recruiting
2. Human resources partner	2. Human resources
3. Talent acquisition specialist	3. Business management
4. Business partner	4. Employee learning & development
5. Human resources business partner	5. Leadership
	6. Digital literacy
	7. Project management
	8. People management
	9. Compensation & benefits
	10. Foreign languages

4 – Product Development	
Jobs	*Skills*
1. Product owner	1. Software testing
2. Quality assurance tester	2. Software Development
3. Agile coach	Life Cycle (SDLC)
4. Software quality assurance engineer	3. Development tools
	4. Project management
5. Product analyst	5. Business management
6. Quality assurance engineer	6. Data storage technologies
	7. Web development
7. Scrum master	8. Manufacturing operations
8. Digital product manager	9. Digital literacy
9. Delivery lead	10. Leadership

5 – Marketing, Sales and Content	
Jobs	*Skills*
1. Social media assistant	1. Digital marketing
2. Growth hacker	2. Social media
3. Customer success specialist	3. Business management
	4. Digital literacy
4. Social media coordinator	5. Advertising
5. Growth manager	6. Product marketing
6. Sales development representative	7. Video
	8. Graphic design
7. Digital marketing specialist	9. Leadership
	10. Writing
8. Commercial sales representative	
9. Business development representative	
10. Customer specialist	

11. Content specialist 12. Content producer 13. Content writer 14. Partnerships specialist 15. Digital specialist 16. Chief commercial officer 17. E-commerce specialist 18. Head of partnerships 19. Commerce manager 20. Head of digital 21. Enterprise account executive 22. Digital marketing consultant 23. Business development specialist 24. Digital marketing manager 25. Chief strategy officer 26. Creative copywriter 27. Chief marketing officer 28. Head of business development	

6 – Care Economy	
Jobs	*Skills*
1. Medical transcriptionists	1. Respiratory therapy
2. Physical therapist aides	2. Caregiving
3. Radiation therapists	3. Sterile procedures/ techniques
4. Athletic trainers	4. Transcription
5. Medical equipment preparers	5. Radiation treatment
6. Veterinary assistants and laboratory animal caretakers	6. Medical dosimetry
	7. Vital signs measurement
	8. Simulation
7. Exercise physiologists	9. Advanced Cardiac Life Support (ACLS)
8. Recreation workers	
9. Personal care aides	10. Radiologic Technology
10. Respiratory therapists	

7 – Green Economy	
Jobs	*Skills*
1. Methane/ landfill gas generation system technicians	1. Digital marketing
	2. Wind turbines
2. Wind turbine service technicians	3. Landfill gas collection
	4. Social media
3. Green marketers	5. Equipment inventory
4. Biofuels processing technicians	6. Solar installation
	7. Health & safety standards
5. Solar energy installation managers	8. Microsoft Power BI
	9. Electrical diagrams/ schematics
6. Water resource specialists	
	10. Email marketing

7. Chief sustainability officers 8. Refuse and recyclable material collectors 9. Sustainability specialists 10. Solar photovoltaic installers 11. Water/wastewater engineers 12. Forest fire inspectors and prevention specialists 13. Fuel cell engineers 14. Nuclear power reactor operators	

LinkedIn 2020 Emerging Jobs Report

On its third annual version and using its proprietary genome metric methodology that aggregates data based on job skills listed rather than degree requirements, LinkedIn's *2020 Emerging Jobs Report* identifies the top fifteen fastest-growing jobs in the United States and the skills associated with them over the last five years. The numbers are based on new platform openings where LinkedIn measures year-over-year growth for each role, ranking the positions by job postings during the same timeframe.

Not surprisingly, artificial intelligence (AI) and data science positions dominate in this ranking, where AI, an infant industry, is already valued at $1.2 trillion. While most skilled workers currently do not work in AI, or probably never will, the segment will impact business models and careers across industries, either by spreading automation or inflicting significant changes upon existing job roles.

Among other trends, the *Emerging Jobs Report* includes the emergence of online learning, the emphasis on human-centric skills for customer service roles in software as a service (SaaS), and a rising demand for robotics engineers, data scientists, and autonomous vehicle AI specialists.

Also, it is worth mentioning that more than 50 percent of listed jobs have robust engineering components, bringing forward again our digital age adage for growth: You either build the stuff that gets sold or you sell the stuff that gets made.

Final highlights include geographical locations for the new jobs. Outside the obvious global city-regions like the San Francisco Bay Area, Chicago, New York, Boston, Seattle, and Los Angeles metro areas, emerging job markets are growing in more affordable, secondary, midsize places, such as Austin, Raleigh-Durham, Pittsburgh, Portland, and Charlotte.

Emerging Jobs Report

Job Role	Annual Growth	Top Skills
1. Artificial intelligence specialist	74%	Machine learning, deep learning, TensorFlow, Python, natural language processing
2. Robotics engineer	40%	Robotic process automation, UiPath, Blue Prism, Automation Anywhere, robotics
3. Data scientist	37%	Machine learning, data science, Python, R, Apache Spark
4. Full stack engineer	35%	React.sj, JavaScript, AngularJS, Cascading Style Sheets (CSS)
5. Site reliability engineer	34%	Amazon Web Services, Ansible, Kubernetes, Docker Products, Terraform
6. Customer success specialist	34%	SaaS, Salesforce, Customer relationships management, account management, customer retention
7. Sales development representative	34%	Salesforce, cold-calling, SaaS, lead generation, sales
8. Data engineer	33%	Apache Spark, Hadoop, Python, Extract/Transform/Load (ETL), Amazon Web Services

9.	Behavioral health technician	32%	Applied Behavioral Analysis, Autism Spectrum Disorders, behavioral health, mental health
10.	Cybersecurity specialist	30%	Cybersecurity, information security, network security, vulnerability assessment
11.	Back end developer	30%	Node.js, JavaScript, Amazon Web Services, Git, MongoDB
12.	Chief revenue officer	28%	Strategic partnerships, start-ups, SaaS, go-to-market strategy, executive engagement
13.	Cloud engineer	27%	Amazon Web Services, cloud computing, Docker Products, Ansible, Jenkins
14.	JavaScript developer	25%	React.js, Node.js AngularJS, JavaScript, Cascading Style Sheets (CSS)
15.	Product owner	24%	Agile Methodologies, Scrum, product management, software development, JIRA

When You Need a Glossary to Read Job Descriptions

If you need a glossary to read digital age skill requirements, don't fret, you're not alone. Tech tools, languages, and applications are evolving so quickly that it's easy to feel overwhelmed. As machine learning encompasses a myriad of business processes, it makes sense to educate yourself about its most popular applications—deep learning and neural networks, to name two, whether you're considering a tech-centric career or not.

There's no question these technologies will turn into extremely lucrative corporate, consulting, and research career areas. Going back to our concept of the AAA strategy, neural networks and deep learning expertise, for instance, will create steppingstones between yourself and this new industry. However, fit, personality, and interest—and, of course, an aptitude for rigorous scientific work—is required. Simultaneously, if you're more of a people person, plenty of non-tech areas will rise in tandem, but to benefit, you'll have to understand them conceptually to keep up with the changes. Above all, you need to know how the transformations translate into demand for new products, new services, and the adoption of new business models.

THE CAREER QUADRANTS

There are four professional quadrants to develop, position, and differentiate yourself in the job market. Joining the right ones is life or death in terms of your overall growth prospects. They are:

High Demand/Low Supply

Ideally, if your vocation, skill set, and personality allow, you want to be in a high demand/low supply quadrant. In this digital age, you become the expert of a rising technology in a booming industry, pure and simple. It doesn't take much other than looking at the LinkedIn and WEF charts here to see where the most lucrative jobs in business, government, and education are heading.

In addition to machine learning and data science, rockin' areas include cybersecurity, data privacy and compliance, cloud, mobile, financial technology (fintech), programmatic advertising, nanotechnologies, 3D printing, virtual reality, and more. An advanced degree in finance, management, computer science, engineering, or applied mathematics is a good start.

Low Demand/High Supply

This is where you don't want to be at all, because you either land here due to technological disruption, outsourcing, or significant changes to your local economy. Draconian public policies, low investments, and severe demographic shifts to regional job markets are some of the factors that push workers to the abyss of the low demand/high supply quadrant when they fail to foresee the changes.

Disintermediation, digitization, and flattening organizations also lead to the quick evaporation of opportunities in a working segment—and not just in manufacturing. More recently, even people in finance—the epitome of a highly educated, white-collar industry—are being displaced by robot-advisors in wealth-management and securities trading. In sum, there's no strategy other than a full overhaul of your skill set when you're here. Outside forces are too powerful to fight. You either build a second career or keep yours as a hobby if there's no financial need and you still love the work.

High Demand/High Supply

Most white-collar, professional service jobs today fall in the high demand/high supply quadrant. While better than low demand/high supply, this quadrant asks you to differentiate yourself through extensive creativity. Grinding on your personal brand and storytelling chops is absolutely key.

Yes, there are opportunities, with some being lucrative and rewarding, but you still must set yourself apart to access legitimate career-accelerating projects. Some strategies include building complementary skills that support market trends, even indirectly. Example: a project manager getting credentials in cybersecurity, a sales manager with a solid track record in SaaS getting certified in Amazon Web Services and Microsoft Azure architectures, or an HR professional gaining credentials on diverse, equitable, and inclusive corporate policies. Other ways to compete include finding growth in lateral industries or building specialization in underserved areas, moving to a different region where the industry is less mature, serving alternative client segments, and moving from corporate to consultancy training roles.

Low Demand/Low Supply

Like the high demand/high supply quadrant, the strategies to compete in the low demand/low supply are grounded on differentiation. However, their intensity varies. The rewards of a micro niche can be astonishing when you're the only, most reputable shop in town, but so are the risks of specializing to the point of no return in a market that's too small to survive. Examples of deep-level expertise include academia, policy formulation, and research. Some renowned academics make seven figures plus as professional speakers, board members, and high-end consultants, while others struggle to find tenured positions at both public and private universities. One scenario is clear: with dwindling public budgets for higher education, especially at state schools, more PhDs are scrambling to find full-time jobs, even as adjunct professors.

While the pathway to glory is painful and prolonged, if there's one quadrant that speaks to who you are—your predilections, inner passions, idiosyncrasies—it is the low demand/low supply. When you deliberately decide to seek a specialization here, you're doing it with your heart. If you're the type who doesn't go with the flow—an artist, a maverick, an intellectual, a purist—there's simply no other place to be.

One of the biggest dilemmas in life is choosing between what you love to do versus what you're good at. Many successful people are pragmatic in picking what they're good at, which may not necessarily be a field they dislike nor a resounding passion. At some point, this is a question you'll have to answer for yourself. For now, here are some insights.

THE CEO OF YOUR CAREER

In the nitty-gritty, what's *really* your best choice for career prosperity? Look at what is trendy to the detriment of vocation and personal desire, or follow your heart and hope for the best?

There are certainly different ways to look at this question, but the answer lies somewhere in the middle, as expected. Peter Drucker, arguably the greatest management guru of all time, argued back in the early 2000s in *Management Challenges for the 21st Century* that workers in the knowledge economy are responsible for managing themselves. What was once the role of major institutions—churches, schools, guilds, unions, corporations—became an individual mission to be carried over a fifty-year productive life span.

Drucker believes that with responsibility comes choice—a phenomenon relatively new in history, since in the past, most people inherited their line of work, for example, being in agriculture, shopkeeping, or priesthood. While a person can only succeed by operating out of strength, most people struggle to find their true talents. One of the questions he poses is, "How do I perform?" Different people have different temperaments that translate into different vocations. For instance, some absorb information by reading or writing. Others make resounding leaps in assimilation and ideation by talking or directly engaging in public discourse.

More than "Are you a reader or listener?" Drucker continues, "Are you a loner, or do you work well with others?" Some people work best as teammates, others as direct subordinates, or entirely alone. To add more colors, there's also the person who does better in decision-making, whereas others excel as talented advisors.

The bottom line is, when you recognize who you are, don't try to change yourself. Instead, improve the way you perform within the boundaries of your natural talents. This thought is at the epicenter of Drucker's thesis because, at heart, a person would know whether she belongs in a large or a small organization or excels in decision-making or supportive roles.

Furthermore, Drucker argues that the societal change that comes with the knowledge economy places much weight on professional success. In the past, careers were made of static contributions that lasted a lifetime. They didn't mean much other than stability and a gold watch in retirement. The only mobility expected with age, and considered normal, was downward mobility. Now, for the first time in history, a person's career is likely to outlive most companies, so in the process, modern workers are the CEOs of their careers and must learn how to navigate complex, infinite possibilities in education and training.

In sum, the bad news: It's easy to get lost amidst tradeoffs and poor choices. The good news: It mostly depends on you. After all, there's no better person to take charge and manage your career with more zeal than yourself.

Final Thoughts

The time to execute your strategy has come. Before we wrap, let's recap your basic commandments as a post-digital divide professional. Take control of your career and fight fiercely for experiential learning that includes high-quality projects and talented people. Remember the 70 percent rule. The right opportunity is the driver. To win, you must operate within the three "must-haves" of career acceleration, 1) the right company, 2) the right boss, and 3) the right projects, because ultimately fit is everything—the only element capable of bringing your whole, authentic self to work daily. Greatness depends on that.

Also, build your competencies in original thinking, people, and communication skills—the cherries on top of the machine age. As data becomes plentiful, the demand for workers with well-rounded interpersonal and cognitive competencies grows. In the end, you want to offer attributes that machines can't—while also working well with them.

Master domain knowledge in a fast-growing field. Some of the most exciting careers require your exact talents and unique touch, but that implies you know exactly who you are—something not so obvious for most people. If you're in the discovery process, I hope some of the strategies in communication and values presented here can ignite your self-awareness. Things to do: Find a mentor, maybe a career coach, complete some personality assessment exercises, get online certifications. Do your homework, and the tools will lead you in the right direction. When you manage your career, more than challenges and occasional roadblocks, you'll find the excitement in discovering your mission and in making long-term contributions.

The future of employment is grounded on a premise that jobs will be fluid, undetermined in duration, and in continuously evolving industries. Ten years ago, Android developer, data scientist, cloud-computer specialist, user experience designer, to name a few, were nonexistent roles.

Today, they're some of the highest-paid, more rewarding occupations at leading technology, professional, and financial service companies. But as technological transformations change career choices, they don't change the timeless principles of success in a human orchestrated world—the same principles shared here to help you win.

Appendix

THE DREAM CAREER CANVAS

Your Digital Age Career
Management Framework

THE DREAM CAREER CANVAS

2 | ### Communication

-Emotionally rational connection
-Negotiation and persuasion
-Written and verbal skills
-The Mood Elevator
-*Emotionally intelligent expression*
-*Empathy*
-*Confidence*
-*Assertiveness*
-Storytelling
-Public speaking
-Whiteboard presentation skills

Original Thinking | **3**

-C.I.A. thinking
-*Critical*
-*Innovative*
-*Analytical*
-Data driven vs. Intuition based decisions
-Pattern recognition
-Positive attitude
-Design thinking
-The AAA principle
-Staying close to the product or the money

1 | ### People and Political Skills

-The three must-haves of career acceleration
-*Right company*
-*Right boss*
-*Right assignments*
-IQ, EQ, PQ mastery
-Understanding human nature
-Joining the HIPO list

4 | ### Leadership

-Ownership mentality
-*Self-Drive*
-*Self-Development*
-*Self-Responsibility*
-Teamwork
-Storytelling
-Leadership-Followership Mastery
-Adaptability
-Strategic Orientation
-Influencing Skills

Technical Domain Level Skills | **5**

-The four skill groups
-*Basic tooling*
-*Behavioral*
-*Generic business*
-*Industry specific*
-The 70 percent rule
-The T-Shaped Individual
-The Future of Jobs
-*Cloud*
-*Mobile*
-*Artificial Intelligence*

People and Political Skills

People and Political skills rule. Relationship skills give you access to the three must-haves of any career acceleration: 1) the right company, 2) the right boss, and 3) the right projects. Together, these elements lead to superior learning and growth. In contrast, you'll be left behind if your only source of competitive advantage is talent, dedication, or academic credentials.

Our educational system is designed to supplement our intelligence quotient (IQ). Growth-oriented professionals, however, are responsible for reaching the next level. That only comes with the mastery of emotional quotient (EQ) and political quotient (PQ). Combined, EQ and PQ capabilities allow you to navigate office politics, culture, and hierarchy, in addition to group norms or informal sources of power that are less obvious and beyond titles.

People and political skills require curiosity and observations about human nature for trustful and respectful relationships to exist. You must do two things to empower your EQ and PQ at work: 1) get a sponsor for exclusive access to mentorship and 2) find projects closely linked to the core business to build your reputation. Somehow, you must gain an official platform for tangible results and career acceleration. In turn, you'll gain a robust network of like-minded individuals for feedback and political alliances.

Your ultimate strategy is to join the hipo, or the high-potentials list—a preferred list of associates reserved for the top 3 to 5 percent of performers in any organization. While hardly advertised, hipo lists do exist, and all decisions on promotions take the buy-in of senior management, who curate them as a balanced score card for candidates.

Ultimately, you'll be a lot closer to leadership, consulting, or entrepreneurial ventures if you master people and political skills. Most successful professionals in business first establish themselves as stellar individual performers when they learn how to manage people and projects well.

Communication

Speaking and writing well are just the basics. To really move the needle, you must communicate in a way that connects and brings people together. Superior communicators establish an emotionally rational connection. They excel in many things, but primarily in negotiation, persuasion, and influencing skills.

What truly makes superior communicators unique is self-awareness. They know exactly who they are and how they best interact. They also know where they and others fit within the four personalities of communication.

The Driver: a natural-born leader who works fast and alone. Drivers take charge and command. They're usually at the helm of projects and groups.

The Expressive: a charismatic, charming, often the most talkative and funny member of a team. Expressives break the ice and love to entertain.

The Analytical: a detail-oriented technician who is adamant about rule-following and procedures. Analyticals keep everyone accountable and on track.

The Amiable: a polite and caring team member. Amiables are integral to keeping the unit. They typically manage conflict and keep people rowing in the same direction.

Not all great communicators are world-class performers, but every world-class performer is a superior communicator. As such, they operate within the penthouse limit of the emotional spectrum, where their mood elevator never lowers to the basement of resentment, frustration, and anger. Instead, their remarks and posture communicate gratitude, insightfulness, and positivity. Furthermore, briefings, meetings, emails, reports, or even casual conversations with superior communicators are packed with confident, assertive communication, which leads to action and results.

Regardless of career stage, any professional benefits from learning storytelling abilities to deliver big-punch, short-whiteboard business presentations. As such, public speaking and presentation skills grease your gears and secure your seat at high-stakes tables.

Original Thinking

Original thinking drives the digital divide. A place in the sun now requires strategic, self-managed, and intelligent choices along the way. To win, professionals need the well-rounded competencies of CIA— critical, innovative, and analytical thinking.

While personality, drive, education, and even talent are plenty, truly original thinking is rare. In a data-flooded world, CIA creates the optimal balance for factual and intuition-based decisions. With it, you separate the essential from noise.

CIA thinkers trace correlations and patterns among items that seem disconnected to the untrained eye. Their scope on context, history, human psychology, technological, and socioeconomic trends promotes better decision making.

CIA thinkers also collect a positive record of better career decisions for themselves as they know exactly who they are and where they're going in life. Anecdotally speaking, luck exists, but at least 80 percent of the results you'll get in life depend on having a positive attitude, resilience, and a strategic mindset. In exchange, none of that exists without critical thinking.

Your thinking abilities allow you to perform at a higher level. Methodologies such as design thinking are great for practical innovations in business. They mesh well with linear thinking competencies developed in numbers, figures, and statistical analysis to measure performance.

Use the Above, Aside, and Ahead (AAA) Principle to "smart" your way out of automation. When navigating your career stages, stay close to the product or the money and work on profit center activities that promote the business at its core.

Keep in mind: The digital age rewards those who build the stuff that gets sold or sell the stuff that gets made. If such areas are not a good fit for you, stick to high-value operational siloes and avoid staff functions. Think strategically. More money is not always the answer.

CIA thinking helps you manage your profile where you objectively take control of your experiences for leveraged growth. With that in mind, focus on things you can control and things that have an impact. Pick projects of visibility in high-growth areas that are future oriented.

Leadership

Responsibilities outweigh authority. The minimum requirement to compete in the digital economy is an ownership mentality—preferably one that allows you to bridge the authority gap between your role and the results you must deliver for greatness. That means you should not only feel responsible, regardless of your role or position, for the outcomes of your team and the organization, but for fundamentally bringing your whole self to work, offering original contributions and innovative forms to solve problems.

The most amazing jobs at the most exciting companies today are reserved for thought leaders—formal or informal organizational leads who work on their self-development and find ways to promote teamwork—often motivated by causes larger than themselves and the creation of legacy contributions that will leave a mark.

Leadership is an evolutionary instrument with key biological and sociological components. Our capacity to mobilize people with abstract thinking and storytelling separates us as a species. Because fiction has the power to spark individual efforts towards large-scale group goals, competent leaders ultimately create myths and sell dreams, harnessing strong collective support as a result.

In the twenty-first century, corporate leaders are essentially rewarded for two things: generating results and building teams. To hit the jackpot, they have two priorities: 1) selling on the merits of big, bold, collective visions and 2) helping others identify their individual purpose in pursuit of such outcomes.

Top leadership roles sit at a rarefied place. Less than 10 percent of professionals reach the C-suite during their careers. While the pathway to the top is harsh, the rewards are big. To board the elevator, you must first understand, then navigate, the social dynamics of leadership-followership profiles, where it's essential to define not only how you operate but how others around you behave. Otherwise, you won't develop working relationships beyond the surface level.

Leadership Profiles

The Technician: a highly analytical, precise, data-driven, logic-oriented leader. Under this relationship dynamic, whether as a leader or follower, your role is to frame meaningful discussions with rationality and solid (preferably numerical, metric-driven) evidence.

The Diplomat: a relationship-oriented leader who seeks to protect harmony and traditional structures. To win over a Diplomat, operate with empathy, social finesse, and civility. Respect their low tolerance for risk while capturing their overall sentiment against conflict, demonstrating alignment with institutional goals without attacking the status quo.

The Driver: a high-energy, goal-oriented, and competitive leader. Drivers are less interested in how you feel and more interested in what you can accomplish. Demonstrate focus, pragmatism, and resilience to extract more of a relationship with this leader.

The Strategist: an exceptional leader who brings forward the best elements of each profile—energy for practical results with group norm appreciation—minus their flaws and excesses. Demonstrate your investment in the vision. Strategists, in general, push for large transformations. As such, they favor strong followers who are willing to fight natural resistance to the new, which often happens with revolutionary, outside-the-box ideas.

Followership Profiles

The Public Relations: a politically attuned follower who's a good reader of the collective mood and generally loyal to the leader. While Public Relations excel in emotional intelligence and communications, these followers usually lack execution and drive. For that reason, they fail to generate tangible results over time.

The Automaton: a disengaged and not remarkably talented follower who sees the job as a paycheck only. While needed for clerical work that's hard to automate, automatons usually don't promote the team's long-term interest and must be replaced or outsourced as they hardly achieve excellence.

The Hired Gun: a talented lone-wolf contributor who's not interested in the relationship dynamics of the workplace. Although typically lacking the political skills to move up the corporate ladder, Hired Guns function well in specific and often strategic areas, and deliver quality work in general.

The Copilot: an ambitious, driven, and politically attuned follower whose contributions seek to raise the overall team's profile and leadership. Copilots are the ideal followers for any excellence-seeking organization. However, Copilots are demanding, and too many of them in the same group can cause teamwork disruptions. They disengage quickly in the absence of growth opportunities.

Red Flags to Bad Leadership

Beware of pitfalls when leading. Self-righteousness is one sign of weakness in leadership. The other is failing to read the environment. A good thermometer of your leadership effectiveness is the analysis of your recent interactions with subordinates. If you frequently think you're right and others are wrong, or if you communicate outside of the penthouse of emotions or even resist tackling difficult conversations, there's a good chance you're displaying poor leadership traits. Conversely, common traits among superior team leaders include adaptability, strategic orientation to win over inevitable and challenging circumstances, and changing management skills to improve processes in motion.

In the long run, the best contribution a leader can make beyond getting results is the forging of the next generation of leaders by passing down a positive legacy and creating a blueprint for a succession pipeline. This requires talent development, coaching, and influencing capabilities. For those who ace this challenge, attractive financial, experiential, and social rewards are the norm.

Technical Domain Level Skills

As much as versatility, well-roundness, and curiosity are important, the concept of T-shaped professionals requires strong domain level expertise. As such, skills to perform at world-class level can be broken down into four groups.

1. Basic tooling skills—or dexterity with the more traditional enterprise software project, product, and collaboration management tools. That includes a minimum of tech savviness for email, reporting, and remote communication activities, including industry-specific skills where certifications or trainings provide recognition so that you will stand out.

2. Universal behavioral skills—or anything that allows you to operate in a professional environment with a minimum of professionalism—from the most basic business etiquette to advanced problem-solving capabilities, effective communication, and cross-collaboration.

3. Multipurpose business skills form another toolkit. They include knowledge and experiences in finance, management, marketing, and design, to capture a tiny fraction of capabilities for the modern

workplace. Most multipurpose skills are transferable across industries.

4. Industry specific skills—mostly technical or ingrained knowledge in core sectors that are valuable to win in key areas, but at the same time are hard to transfer.

The 70 Percent Rule

This is an invisible principle followed by recruiters and senior managers when designing compensation packages. It reveals that for every dollar paid in remuneration, $0.70 should correspond to your practical knowledge experiences and how the market values them. The remaining 30 percent reflects formal education and training credentials. In sum, your compensation is a direct byproduct of your *practical* career experiences where better experiences (and projects) mean more money. With this ratio, your project portfolio functions as the primary vehicle to sell your tradeable skills.

The digital economy has several career tracks to offer. Broad areas of specialization include digital product creation, design, media, marketing, and branding. Additionally, credentials are surpassing degrees in high-growth, lucrative areas, mostly in segments driving the future of work, defined by the WEF as cloud, mobile, artificial intelligence, and big data. Inside those areas, the WEF defines seven promising career clusters where top economic investment will be concentrated. They are:

1. Data and AI
2. Engineering and cloud computing

3. People and culture
4. Product development
5. Marketing, sales & content
6. Care economy
7. Green economy

To choose a cluster, it's best to observe the classic career quadrants before positioning yourself for the job market.

- High demand-low supply
  ○ High-paid STEM-related careers
- Low demand-high supply
  ○ Low paid clerical work
- High demand-high supply
  ○ Low- or high-paid white-collar office roles
- Low demand-low supply
  ○ Low- or high-paid ultra-niched careers

Passion vs. talent is a quintessential career dilemma everyone faces at some point. The answer is not clear. As the CEO of your career, the right balance is something you'll have to define for yourself. With companies too busy fighting for survival to attend to employee development, the responsibility to manage your career is yours. As your personal career CEO, your critical mission is defined as follows.

- Define your strengths before you look for fit.
- Fight fiercely for great opportunities, then deliver.
- Master domain knowledge in a fast-growing field.
- Find a mentor or coach.
- Complete personality assessments.
- Seek online certifications and trainings.

Endnotes

1   Marc Ethier, "What It Now Costs to Get to a Top-25 MBA Degree," *Poets and Quants* (Nov. 2, 2020), https://poetsand-quants.com/2020/11/02/covid-slows-but-cant-stop-the-rising-cost-of-a-top-25-u-s-mba-program/.

2   Carl Benedikt Frey and Michael A. Osborne, "The Future of Employment: How Susceptible Are Jobs to Computerization?" Oxford Martin School (Sept. 17, 2013), https://www.oxfordmartin.ox.ac.uk/downloads/academic/future-of-employment.pdf.

3   Jim Resnik, "One Monthly Fee, a Catalog of Porsches," *New York Times*, June 18, 2020,https://www.nytimes.com/2020/06/18/business/porsche-drive-subscription-service.html.

4   Elaine Low, "Netflix Reveals $17 Billion in Content Spending in Fiscal 2021," *Variety*, April 20, 2021, https://variety.com/2021/tv/news/netflix-2021-content-spend-17-billion-1234955953/

5   Erik Brynjolfsson and Andrew McAfee, *The Second Machine Age: Work, Progress, and Prosperity an a Time of Brilliant Technologies* (New York: Norton & Company, 2014).

6   Peter Cappelli, "HR for Neophytes," *Harvard Business Review*, October 2013.

7   Douglas A. Ready, "Are You a High Potential?" *Harvard Business Review*, June 2010, https://hbr.org/2010/06/are-you-a-high-potential.

8   John C. Maxwell, *Everyone Communicates, Few Connect* (Nashville: Thomas Nelson Inc, 2010).

9   Daniel Goleman, *Working with Emotional Intelligence* (New York: Bantam, 2000).

10   Travis Bradberry and Jean Greaves, *Emotional Intelligence 2.0* (San Diego: Talent Smart, 2009).

11   Larry Senn, *The Mood Elevator: Take Charge of your Feelings, Become a Better You.* Oakland: Berret-Koehler Publishers Inc., 2017.

12   Maxwell, *Everyone Communicates.*

13   Albert Mehrabian, *Silent Messages* (Boston: Cengage Learning, 1971).

14   Maxwell, *Everyone Communicates.*

15   Carmine Gallo, "The Art of Persuasion Hasn't Changed in 2,000 Years," *Harvard Business Review*, June 2020.

16   Gallo, "The Art of Persuasion."

17   Frey and Osborne, "The Future of Employment: How Susceptible Are Jobs to Computerization?"

18   Jeff Kauflin,. "The Best and Worst Master's Degrees for Jobs in 2017." *Forbes Magazine*, September 7, 2017.

19   T. H. Davenport & J. Kirby, "Beyond Automation—Strategies for Remaining Gainfully Employed in an Era of Very Smart Machines," *Harvard Business Review*, June 2015.

20   Ellen McGirt. "The Black Ceiling: Why African-American Women Aren't Making it to the Top in Corporate America. *Fortune.* September 27, 2017. https://fortune.com/2017/09/27/black-female-ceos-fortune-500-companies/

21   Michael Shinagel, "The Paradox of Leadership," Professional Development, Harvard Division of Continuing Education, July 3, 2013, https://professional.dce.harvard.edu/blog/the-paradox-of-leadership/

22   R. L. Hughes, R. C. Ginnett, & G. J. Curphy, *Leadership: Enhancing the Lessons of Experience* (New York: Mcgraw-Hill Education, 2015).

23   Rachel Feintzeig, "Want to Be CEO? Stand Tall," *Wall Street Journal*, June 9, 2014.

24   Cappelli, "HR for Neophytes."

25   Cappelli, "HR for Neophytes."

26   Jim Clifton. *The Coming Jobs War.* (New York: Gallup Press, 2011).

27   Jennifer Elias and Megan Graham, "How Google's $150 Billion Advertising Business Works," CNBC, May 18, 2021, https://www.cnbc.com/2021/05/18/how-does-google-make-money-advertising-business-breakdown-.html

Selected Bibliography

Aten, Jason. "The 12 Most Popular Workplace Software Apps 2020."*Inc. Magazine,* January 28, 2020.

Bradberry, Travis., and Jean Greaves. *Emotional Intelligence 2.0.* San Diego: Talent Smart, 2009.

Brynjolfsson, Erik., and Andrew McAfee. *The Second Machine Age: Work, Progress, and Prosperity in a Time of Brilliant Technologies.* New York: Norton & Company, 2014.

Buckingham, Marcus., and Ashley Goodall. "Reinventing Performance Management." *Harvard Business Review,* April 2015.

Buckingham, Virginia. "How to Recover When Your Career Gets Derailed." *Harvard Business Review,* April 2020.

Cappelli, Peter. "HR for Neophytes." *Harvard Business Review,* October 2019.

Chopra, Vineet., and Sanjay Saint. "What Mentors Wish Their Mentees Knew." *Harvard Business Review,* November 2017.

Clifton, Jim. *The Coming Jobs War.* New York: Gallup Press, 2011.

Davenport, Thomas H., and Julia Kirby. "Beyond Automation—Strategies for Remaining Gainfully Employed in an Era of Very Smart Machines." *Harvard Business Review,* June 2015.

Davis, Alyssa., and Kyley McGeeney. "In U.S., Employment Most Linked to Being Depression Free." *Gallup-Healthways Well-Being Index,* August 23, 2013.

Drucker, Peter. *Management Challenges for the 21st Century.* New York: Harper Collins, 2019.

Fernandez-Ardoz, Claudio. "21st-Century Talent Spotting: Why Potential Now Trumps Brains, Experience and Competencies." *Harvard Business Review,* June 2014.

Frey, Carl Benedikt., and Michael A. Osborne. "The Future of Employment: How Susceptible are Jobs to Computerization?". Oxford Martin School, University of Oxford. September 2013.

Gallo, Carmine. "The Art of Persuasion Hasn't Changed in 2,000 Years." *Harvard Business Review,* June 2018.

Galloway, Scott. *The Four: The Hidden DNA of Amazon, Apple, Facebook, and Google.* New York: Penguin Random House, 2017.

Gardner, Howard. *Changing Minds.* Boston: Harvard Business School, 2006.

George, Bill., Peter Sims, Andrew N. McLean, and Diana Mayer. "Discovering Your Authentic Leadership." *Harvard Business Review,* February 2007.

Goffee, Robert., and Gareth Jones. "Why Should Anyone Be Led by You?" *Harvard Business Review,* October 2000.

Goleman, Daniel. *Working with Emotional Intelligence.* New York: Bantam Books, 1998.

Goleman, Daniel. "What Makes a Leader?" *Harvard Business Review,* January 2004.

Griffin, Tren. "12 Things About Product-Market-Fit." *Future.* February 18, 2017. https://future.a16z.com/about-product-market-fit/.

Hamilton, Cheryl., and Tony L. Kroll. *Communicating for Results; A Guide for Business and the Professionals.* Boston: Cengage Learning, 2017.

Hamlin, Sonya. *How to Talk So People Listen: Connecting in Today's Workplace*. New York City: Harper Business, 1988.

Harari, Yuval Noah. *Sapiens: A Brief History of Humankind*. New York: HarperCollins Publishers, 2014.

Harvard Business Review. *On Leadership*. Boston: Harvard Business Review Press, 2011.

Hughes, Richard L., Robert C. Ginnett, and Gordon J. Curphy. *Leadership, Enhancing the Lessons of Experience*. New York: Mcgraw-Hill Education, 2015.

Ibarra, Herminia. "Reinventing Your Career in the Time of Coronavirus." *Harvard Business Review*, April 2020.

Kauflin, Jeff. "The Best and Worst Master's Degrees for Jobs in 2017." *Forbes Magazine*, September 7, 2017.

Keen, Andrew. *The Internet is Not the Answer*. New York: Atlantic Monthly Press, 2016.

Kelley, Tom., and David Kelley. *Creative Confidence, Unleashing the Creative Potential within Us All*. New York: Crown Business, 2013.

Knight, Rebecca. "How to Tell If a Company's Culture is Right for You." *Harvard Business Review*, November, 2017.

Lencioni, Patrick. *Overcoming The Five Dysfuctions of a Team.* San Francisco: Jossey-Bass, 2005.

Marks, Michell Lee., Phillip Mirvis, and Ron Ashkenas. "Rebounding from Career Setbacks." *Harvard Business Review,* October 2014.

Marr, Bernard. *The Intelligence Revolution, Transforming Your Business with A.I.* New York City: Kogan Page, 2020.

Maxwell, John C. *Everyone Communicates, Few Connect.* Nashville: Thomas Nelson, 2011.

McGirt, Ellen. "The Black Ceiling: Why African-American Women Aren't Making it to the Top in Corporate America. *Fortune Magazine.* September 27, 2017.

Mehrabian, Albert. *Silent Messages.* Boston: Cengage Learning, 1971.

Merril, David W., and Roger H. Reid. *Personal Styles and Effective Performance.* Boca Raton: CRC Press LLC, 1999.

Meyer, Erin. *The Culture Map: Breaking Through the Invisible Boundaries of Global Business.* New York: Public Affairs, 2014.

Munk, Cheryl Winokur. "Six Theories on Why Fast-Growing Startups Seem to Be Disapeearing." *The Wall Street Journal,* May 12, 2020.

Nadherny, Chris. *The Proactive Executive.* Mount Pleasant, SC: Bublish Inc., 2017

Owen, Jo. *Mobile MBA, 112 Skills to Take You Further, Faster.* London: Financial Times Prentice Hall, Pearson Education Limited, 2011.

Peppercorn, Susan. "7 Questions to Raise Immediatelly after You're Laid Off." *Harvard Business Review,* March 2020.

Ready, Douglas A., Jay A. Conger, and Linda A. Hill. "Are You a High Potential?" *Harvard Business Review,* June 2010.

Rifkin, Jeremy. *The Age of Access: The New Culture of Hypercapitalism, Where All of Life Is a Paid-For Experience.* New York: Penguin Putnam Inc., 2001.

Rooke, David., and William R. Torbert. "Seven Transformations of Leadership." *Harvard Business Review,* April 2005.

Senn, Larry. *The Mood Elevator: Take Charge of your Feelings, Become a Better You.* Oakland: Berret-Koehler Publishers Inc., 2017.

Singh, Aditya. "Deep Learning Will Radically Change the Ways We Interact with Technology." *Harvard Business Review,* January 2017.

Steinberger, Michael. "What is the Stock Market Even for Anymore?" *The New York Times*, May 26, 2020.

Weissman, Jerry. *Presenting to Win. The Art of Telling Your Story.* New Jersey: Pearson Education Inc., 2009.

Wilson, H. James., Paul R. Daugherty, and Chase Davenport. "The Future of AI Will be About Less Data, Not More." *Harvard Business Review,* January 2019.

Zenger, Jack., and Joseph Folkman. "Why the Most Productive People Don't Always Make the Best Managers." *Harvard Business Review*, April 2018.

Notes

1   Marc Ethier, "What It Now Costs to Get to a Top-25 MBA Degree," *Poets and Quants* (Nov. 2, 2020), https://poetsand-quants.com/2020/11/02/covid-slows-but-cant-stop-the-rising-cost-of-a-top-25-u-s-mba-program/.

2   Carl Benedikt Frey and Michael A. Osborne, "The Future of Employment: How Susceptible Are Jobs to Computerization?" Oxford Martin School (Sept. 17, 2013), https://www.oxfordmar-tin.ox.ac.uk/downloads/academic/future-of-employment.pdf.

3   Jim Resnik, "One Monthly Fee, a Catalog of Porsches," *New York Times*, June 18, 2020, https://www.nytimes.com/2020/06/18/business/porsche-drive-subscription-service.html.

4   Elaine Low, "Netflix Reveals $17 Billion in Content Spending in Fiscal 2021," *Variety*, April 20, 2021, https://variety.com/2021/tv/news/netflix-2021-content-spend-17-billion-1234955953/

5   Erik Brynjolfsson and Andrew McAfee, *The Second Machine Age: Work, Progress, and Prosperity an a Time of Brilliant Technologies* (New York: Norton & Company, 2014).

6   Peter Cappelli, "HR for Neophytes," *Harvard Business Review*, October 2013.

7   Douglas A. Ready, "Are You a High Potential?" *Harvard Business Review*, June 2010, https://hbr.org/2010/06/are-you-a-high-potential.

8   John C. Maxwell, *Everyone Communicates, Few Connect* (Nashville: Thomas Nelson Inc, 2010).

9   Daniel Goleman, *Working with Emotional Intelligence* (New York: Bantam, 2000).

10 Travis Bradberry and Jean Greaves, *Emotional Intelligence 2.0* (San Diego: Talent Smart, 2009).

11 Larry Senn, The Mood Elevator: *Take Charge of your Feelings, Become a Better You.* Oakland: Berret Koehler Publishers Inc., 2017.

12 Maxwell, *Everyone Communicates.*

13 Albert Mehrabian, *Silent Messages* (Boston: Cengage Learning, 1971).

14 Maxwell, *Everyone Communicates.*

15 Carmine Gallo, "The Art of Persuasion Hasn't Changed in 2,000 Years," *Harvard Business Review*, June 2020.

16 Gallo, "The Art of Persuasion."

17 Benedikt and Osborne, "The Future of Employment: How Susceptible Are Jobs to Computerization?"

18 Jeff Kauflin. "The Best and Worst Master's Degrees for Jobs in 2017." *Forbes Magazine,* September 7, 2017.

19 T. H. Davenport & J. Kirby, "Beyond Automation—Strategies for Remaining Gainfully Employed in an Era of Very Smart Machines," *Harvard Business Review*, June 2015.

20 Ellen McGirt. "The Black Ceiling: Why African-American Women Aren't Making it to the Top in Corporate America. *Fortune.* September 27, 2017. https://fortune.com/2017/09/27/black-female-ceos-fortune-500-companies/

21 Michael Shinagel, "The Paradox of Leadership," Professional Development, Harvard Division of Continuing Education, July 3, 2013. https://professional.dce.harvard.edu/blog/the-paradox-of-leadership/

22 R. L. Hughes, R. C. Ginnett, & G. J. Curphy, *Leadership: Enhancing the Lessons of Experience* (New York: Mcgraw-Hill Education, 2015).

23 Rachel Feintzeig, "Want to Be CEO? Stand Tall," *Wall Street Journal*, June 9, 2014.

24 Peter Cappelli, "HR for Neophytes."

25 Cappelli, "HR for Neophytes."

26 Jim Clifton. *The Coming Jobs War*. (New York: Gallup Press, 2011).

27 Jennifer Elias and Megan Graham, "How Google's $150 Billion Advertising Business Works," CNBC, May 18, 2021, https://www.cnbc.com/2021/05/18/how-does-google-make-money-advertising-business-breakdown-.html.

CPSIA information can be obtained
at www.ICGtesting.com
Printed in the USA
BVHW030143081022
648929BV00013B/1569